Comforting Thoughts...
To Soothe Our Souls and Lift Our Spirits

By Dr. George Mathison

Dedicatory Page

This book is lovingly dedicated to three men who make up our executive staff here at Auburn United Methodist Church. They are not only colleagues in ministry who share with me a theological compatibility, a common vision for our church and a deep love for the Christ whom we serve; but most importantly they are dear friends and brothers in Christ who daily exemplify for me and our church family what it means to effectively be in ministry and provide leadership for this community of faith. I, as the senior minister of AUMC, am so blessed to share this ministry with them: John Wingfield, Charles Cummings and John Fox. In them, I daily see the incarnation and manifestation of this book as they indeed **comfort** my faith, **soothe** my soul and **lift** my **spirit**. Thank you John, Charles and John for your friendship and for all you mean to our church—and to you, this book is humbly dedicated.

This book is also dedicated to Reverend Sandy Simmons who, when we began this ministry together, kindly opened to me his home and parsonage in Banks, Alabama, when I served the Perote Charge, and I did not have a parsonage. Truth be known, I did not have much of anything. We began this ministerial journey together, and over the years he has continued to open his heart to me and countless others through the precious gift of friendship.

Preface

As I write these lines and begin to put these *thoughts* together in book form, I am in the process of preaching a series of sermons on the theme of grief in our church here at Auburn United Methodist Church. AUMC is a great university church of over 4,000 members located one block from Auburn University. I shared with my congregation that I am preaching these sermons for two reasons:

One, the future is very uncertain. For all of us, sooner or later, the dreaded Pale Horseman of Death is going to visit us. Paul wrote to the Hebrew Christians and said, "It is appointed unto man once to die." The visit of "The Horseman" and that divine appointment will come sooner or later, and I've found that it inevitably and invariably comes much, much sooner. These sermons are to help prepare us for that time.

Two, we have had an unprecedented number of deaths in our church over the past several months. Many of our loved ones within our church family have recently died. I have personally been with several families in the hospital ICU and at Bethany House (a wonderful hospice care facility in our community), and I've ministered to them and hurt with them as I saw and experienced their loved ones lay down their crosses and take up their crowns. It is an emotional experience for a pastor to be with a family at the time of the death of a dear family member. As I shared with my congregation, quite frankly, *many* of our people are hurting and grieving. One man said to me, "Dr. Mathison, it has been several weeks since the funeral, and yet it hurts now more than it did then. How do I handle this? How do I grieve properly?" These sermons on grief are an attempt to answer these questions, especially the chapter on *Jairus: Struggling With Grief*, as it is a contemplative study directed inwardly to strengthen and challenge the faith of our congregation. Perhaps I should point out that this chapter on grief is one of several taken from a number of sermons I recently preached on the theme, *Good People in Bad Places.* There were twenty-five sermons in this series, and I've carefully selected the ones that I feel directly address the theme of this book and the ***bad places*** where ***good people*** find themselves in this day in which we live. These chapters comprise the **First Section** of this book.

The **Second Section** of this book is a compilation of four sermons I preached on the theme, ***Biblical Principles by Which I Daily Live.*** It is my prayer that the first part of the book will help us work through our grief, find peace in our hearts and a solace for our souls. But then, we must engage in the big business of living life each day. That is where the second part of this book comes into play. For after we have worked through our grief, I want to show you four scriptural principles that can help you live a spiritually victorious life every day. I begin every day reciting these principles and reflecting upon their application for my life through the day. They are indeed, for me, the four scriptural keys that unlock the door for a happy and fulfilling day. I remember when I was working on my Doctorate in the Sewanee–Vanderbilt Joint Doctoral program, one of the first courses I took was a "Ministry Seminar," and in that class we were required to write out our philosophy of ministry. I remember my paper was very academic and cerebral as I sought to define my understanding of Christian Ministry. Today, thirty-five years later, my philosophy of ministry is much simpler. My philosophy of life is far less complex. At this point in my ministry, these are the four principles that not only govern my philosophy of ministry, but more importantly, my life as a person. Because these biblical principles provide the parameters of my life and give inspiration and motivation to my ministry, I've chosen to include them in this book as they provide the foundation for my life. It is my prayer that you will allow these principles to become the foundation upon which you build your Christian life each day.

The **Third Section** is a compilation of sermons that can give continued strength, comfort, guidance and solace as we live life each day.

At this juncture, it is important for me to point out that this book is not written for an academic classroom setting. It is not a deep theological treatise for scholars to discuss nearly as much as a compilation of simple sermons for the average lay person to use in his spiritual journey. These are simple sermons that I preached over several Sundays to my congregation. Ministers have different ways of preparing and delivering sermons. My way is to set aside Wednesday and Friday mornings of each week. This is time that I sacredly guard because I consider these mornings the most important time of my week. Beginning at four o'clock in the morning, I go into my study and immerse myself in the Greek New Testament. I then spend many hours in research and preparation. All of these efforts are undergirded by deep and contemplative prayer. *Then on Sunday, without any notes, I simply stand before my people and preach from the overflow of my heart. That is how the sermons in this book were preached. These sermons were then taken from the CD's of the sermons on those particular Sundays, and they were transcribed and put into written form for the first time. They are found in this book exactly as they were preached to my people. In my previous books of sermons, I have edited them and emendated them to accommodate a reading audience. This book is different. These sermons, with no editing, are printed exactly as they were preached in our church. So as you read these sermons, in your mind just imagine yourself sitting in our congregation at AUMC and I am standing before you preaching without any notes from the very depths of my heart—especially to you.*

In one of the chapters, I quote Henri Nouwen as he says, "Our life is full of brokenness—broken relationships, broken promises, and broken experiences. How can we live with that brokenness without becoming bitter and resentful except by returning again and again to God's faithful presence in our lives?" Thus, it is against the background of this spirit and wisdom of Dr. Nouwen that I present and share this simple book with you with the prayer that we will return "again to God's faithful presence in our lives," and I pray these **thoughts** will indeed bring *comfort* by *soothing our souls* and *lifting our spirits*.

Dr. George Mathison
Senior Minister
Auburn United Methodist Church

A very special thank you to Michelle Morrison, Jill Perry, Chris Kelsey and Retha Cole for their assistance with this project.

If you would like a DVD of any one, or all, of the sermons in this book as they were preached in worship services at Auburn United Methodist Church, please contact Michelle Morrison at AUMC, by calling 334-826-8800. Please identify the Worship Service by the sermon title.

Sanctuary Choir coming in.

The 11:00 a.m. Traditional Service.

The 9:30 a.m. Contemporary Service.

The 11:00 a.m. Resonate Service.

Table of Contents

Other Books by Dr. Mathison

Positive Thoughts...From a Perfect Season

Winning Thoughts...For Any Season of Life

Inspirational Thoughts...For Each Season of the Year

Encouraging Thoughts...For the Good and Bad Seasons of Life

Prayerful Thoughts...For Daily Living

Healing Thoughts...To Mend Hurting Hearts

Peaceful Thoughts...For the Stormy Seasons of Life

Section I

Good People in Bad Places

Chapter 1

Elijah: Sitting Under the Juniper Tree of Discouragement

*"He came to a juniper or broom tree, sat down under it and
prayed that he might die. 'I have had enough, Lord,' he said.
'Take my life; I am no better than my ancestors.'"*
I Kings 19:4
I Kings 19:3-5
Good People in Bad Places

With this message I want to begin a series of sermons on
the theme: ***Good People in Bad Places***.

Sometimes good Christian people have a way of getting
into wrong and bad places. Sometimes we find ourselves in
places where we are not supposed to be.

I remember some time ago I was speaking at a meeting at
a hotel in Atlanta, Georgia. It was a corporate meeting and I was
giving a motivational speech. Because of the large gathering of
people, I was a little nervous. I stepped inside the door of the
restroom to gather my thoughts and go over my message. While I
was standing there, a person walked up to me, saw my name tag
and said, "Dr. Mathison, you're not nervous, are you?" I said,
"Why no, why would you think that?" The person said, "Because
you are in the ladies room!" Yes, sometimes right people have a
way of being in wrong places.

Now the reason that good people find themselves in bad
places is because we're not perfect. In the Sermon on the Mount,
Jesus said in Matthew 5:48, *"Be perfect even as your Father in
heaven is perfect."* That is the goal and that is the ideal for which
we are striving, but along the way we are going to make mistakes.

You see, there are three steps in the spiritual process. ***One***,
there is <u>salvation</u> where we come to know Jesus Christ. ***Two***,
there is <u>sanctification</u> where we experience the fullness of the
Holy Spirit and grow in Jesus Christ. And ***three***, there is
<u>glorification</u> that we will experience someday when we are

3

perfected and we become like Jesus Christ, for John said in one of his letters, *"In that day, we shall see Him as He is and we shall be like Him."*

But in the process, right people are going to get into wrong places. Good people are going to get into bad places, and when I speak of these places, I am not referring to physical places, but I am alluding to mental and emotional and spiritual places.

As you study the Bible, it is interesting to discover that some of the greatest figures in the Bible found themselves in these places. Some good men and women got into some very bad places.

What I want to do in this series of sermons is share with you the lives of several of these good people who got into bad places; and the way we are going to do it is to lift up certain biblical characters, study the scriptural background from where their stories are taken, and then make a relevant application of their lives and their problems for us today.

In this first message, I want us to look at Elijah. Elijah was a good man, but he found himself in a bad place. He was a right person who ended up in a wrong place.

Elijah's story is told in I Kings 19, and I especially want us to notice verses 3-5.

I remember when we were in the Holy Land. Our tour bus left the Valley of Jezreel, and we were en route to Haifa. I remember as we pulled into that city our guide pointed to a huge mountain sloping into the Mediterranean Sea. I never will forget how our guide told us that the mountain was Mt. Carmel. He then refreshed our memories and told us again of how Elijah used that mountain as a pulpit, and it was there also that he defeated the Prophets of Baal, and he won a great victory.

It was a time of great exultation for Elijah and the people of God.

And then the news reached Jezebel, the wicked Queen, and she became violently angry. She sent a message to Elijah

4

saying, *"You have slain my prophets. Now I will do the same to you. By this time tomorrow, you will join them in death."*

That powerful threat by the Queen sent tremors of fear through Elijah. He forgot about the victory, and the only thing he could think about was that violent threat by Queen Jezebel. Elijah became so disconcerted that he started running from Mt. Carmel, and he did not stop until he reached Beersheba. When he got there, our text tells us that he was so exhausted and frightened and intimidated that he sat down under a juniper tree, or a broom tree, and he entered into a severe state of despair and discouragement and despondency as he said, "Lord, just let me die."

Now, Brother Elijah lived in a distant yesterday, but he has a lot of twenty-first century cousins today. So many people today are dismayed, discouraged, despondent and despairing. You would be surprised at how many people are sitting under the juniper tree of discouragement in this modern day in which we live. You would be surprised at how many disappointed and despondent people there are in this worship service today. You would be surprised at how many pillows last night were wet with tears of discouragement that this world will never know anything about.

A minister preached in a church in a northern state, and he said that the following week he received a letter from a woman who was in that service. With the letter, she enclosed this poem:

I cannot find the stars tonight,
So black the sky bends over;
I cannot hear the happy winds
That glean the fields of clover.

I cannot see the bladed grass,
So dark the night tide going;
I cannot hear the happy leaves
Singing their songs of growing.

But somewhere, where the shadows end,
Begins a newer story;
And somewhere past horizon's rim
The day is making glory.

And surely in the soundless dark
The honey—saps are flowing;
And somewhere waits the perfect bloom
A gracious hand's bestowing.

At the bottom of the poem, this dear lady wrote these words, "I do not know poetry, but I do know that these verses hold a truth that gives me strength and hope for courageous living when I am discouraged."

Now that lady didn't realize it, but her thoughts were a perfect description of Elijah sitting under the juniper tree, and they were also looking into what John of the Cross calls "the dark night of the soul."

This experience is what the Church Fathers called "sloth," which is one of the seven deadly sins.

It is a mood in which a person feels spiritually dry and mentally depleted. God seems far away, and a person condemns and dislikes himself and feels all alone and does not know where to find the power to pull himself together.

What is interesting is that this is an experience that comes to deeply religious people.

Elijah is perhaps the perfect picture of this as he is sitting under the ***Juniper Tree***.

Jeremiah the Prophet experienced it when he wrote, *"Why is my pain perpetual and my wound incurable that refuses to be healed. Will you be to me as a deceitful brook, as waters that fail."*

Job also knew this deep pain as he wrote, *"How long will you look away from me?"*

David experienced this as he said in Psalm 69:1-3, *"The waters are covering me. I am sinking."*

6

Again the Psalmist knew this pain when he cried out, *"How long, Oh God, will You hide Your face from me?"*

Even Jesus experienced it as He cried upon the cross, *"My God, My God, why have You forsaken Me?"*

And yes, again, Elijah and these Biblical Saints have a lot of twenty-first century kinfolks with this same problem.

A book that has helped me very much in addressing this bad place is the volume entitled ***The Dark Night of the Soul*** by John of the Cross. This book is one of the great spiritual classics of the Church.

John of the Cross was raised under very poor circumstances. He later attended a Jesuit school and was ordained at the age of twenty-five. In 1658, along with Teresa of Avila, he organized the Order of the Barefooted Carmelites, a religious movement that deeply improved the spiritual life of Spain and France in the seventeenth century.

In this classic writing, ***The Dark Night of the Soul***, John of the Cross describes the dryness, sadness and the loneliness of a person's spirit, and he shows how this terrifying feeling can be overcome.

When we like Elijah find ourselves under the juniper tree and feel this inner desolation, despondency and despair, John suggests four helpful steps. I have taken his thoughts, and I have alliterated them, modernized them and couched them in contemporary terminology so we can better understand them.

When we find ourselves, like Elijah, under the juniper tree of discouragement, and when we find ourselves in "the dark night of the soul," we need to take four simple steps as suggested by John of the Cross. We need to:

I.   **Realize**
II.   **Rest**
III.   **Recognize**
IV.   **Refocus**
V.   **Remind**

I. Realize

The first step John suggests is that we realize we are facing the problem of despondency and discouragement. We must realize where we are. You see, it is very difficult to solve a problem if you do not know a problem is existent. This is the starting point.

The first step in Alcoholics Anonymous, Gamblers Anonymous, and Narcotics Anonymous is the **realization** of the problem and a willingness to be helped.

And so, one, **realize** where you are and have within you a desire to overcome your discouragement and get out from under that juniper tree.

II. Rest

John then suggests that we not try too hard to rise above it at first, but simply to **rest** our bodies and minds and souls and spirits.

It is interesting to note that this is precisely what Elijah did when he was under the juniper tree. Yes, he realized where he was, but our text also tells us that he **rested** and became relaxed.

It is important for us to understand that in the resting process, we need to fill our minds with Scriptures that pertain to rest and peace.

I think of several of them. Isaiah said, *"God will keep us in perfect peace when our minds are stayed upon Him."*

The Psalmist said, *"Be still and know that I am God."*

David wrote, *"The Lord is my shepherd, I shall not want. He makes me to lie down in green pastures, He leads me beside the still waters. He restores my soul."* You see, when we are discouraged and under the juniper tree, it means that our spirits are shattered, and with God's healing grace they must be restored. David reminds us that it is God, the Good Shepherd, who restores our souls.

And then I think of the words of Jesus when He said, *"Come to Me all who labor and are heavy laden, and I will give you rest,"* and John of the Cross suggests that we combine this restful attitude with thoughts on the life and suffering of Christ.

III.   Recognize

It is absolutely imperative for us to **recognize** what we can change and what we cannot change.

We need to pray the prayer of Reinhold Niebuhr when he said,

Lord, grant me the serenity to accept
The things I cannot change;
The courage to change the things I can;
And the wisdom to know the difference.

Recognize what you cannot change. There are many things you cannot change. You cannot change the past. The past is gone. You have no control over what happened yesterday. You cannot control how people act or what they do. The only thing you can control is your attitude towards them and how you will act and respond.

You see, so much of our discouragement and depression are caused by a desire to change that which is unchangeable. Recognize what you cannot change, and say along with the Apostle Paul, *"This one thing I do, forgetting what is behind, I press toward the mark for the prize for the high calling of God in Christ Jesus."*

IV.   Refocus

Refocus your thoughts, your attitudes and your thinking pattern. The writer of Proverbs said, "As you think within your heart, so you are." Our thoughts determine our actions, and our actions define who we are as people.

We need to understand that much of our discouragement

is caused by selfishness and fear. We must learn to get out of ourselves and live above our fears; and the way we do that is to focus our thinking upon something bigger than ourselves. One person said, "Life is just too much trouble unless you can live for something bigger than yourself."

I know that sometimes when I tend to be discouraged or despondent or down, I immediately **refocus** my thoughts and get busy. Now I don't recommend this to everybody, but usually if I'm feeling a little down in the dumps, I will get my Greek New Testament and begin to study it. I start to conjugate verbs and go through noun declensions, and as I do it, I get ideas for sermons, and because I love my people so much, I know I am getting sermon ideas that will help them, and this blesses me. The bi-product of that study is that my thoughts are focused upon my work, and thus the despondency and depression are eliminated and I begin to have a positive and healthy attitude.

I think about Elijah, and as long as he was looking back at the past, he was despondent. When he looked with fear to the future, he was discouraged. But when he filled his mind with positive thoughts, rested, **refocused**, and looked up, it was then that he became productive, and he became one of the great Prophets of the Old Testament.

V.   Remind

And to these four aids by John of the Cross, I have added a fifth, and the fifth is to **remind** yourself of how much God loves you. You need to remember you are His child and He cares about you and loves you, and He wants to help you get out from under the juniper tree and move beyond "the dark night of the soul" into the salubrious sunshine of the bright day.

One week ago yesterday I did the funeral service for a sweet little baby boy. He was the son of one of the fine fire fighters in our community here in Auburn. I never will forget how I looked into the grieving faces of that dear mother and father. All through the service, I could sense their deep love and affection for

10

their little baby boy. I shared with them that I knew how much they loved their little boy, and then I told them that they needed to realize an even greater truth, and that is that God loves them infinitely more. They are His children, and God loves and cares about them, and just as He helped them get through that difficult time, so His care for you is just as great, and He wants to help you...and how we need to be **reminded** of God's care and love for us.

In closing, I want us to **remind** ourselves of God's love and care for us. One of the great hymns of the faith is *God Will Take Care of You*. I want us to remain seated as we prayerfully and reflectively sing the first three verses, and then we will stand on the fourth verse. These verses **remind** us of a great truth. In the stillness of this moment, allow this truth to fill your heart, soul and mind.

Be not dismayed whate're betide,
God will take care of you;
Beneath his wings of love abide,
God will take care of you.

Through days of toil when heart doth fail,
God will take care of you;
When dangers fierce your path assail,
God will take care of you.

All you may need he will provide,
God will take care of you;
Nothing you ask will be denied,
God will take care of you.

No matter what may be the test,
God will take care of you;
Lean, weary one, upon his breast,
God will take care of you.

Chapter 2

The Twelve Disciples: Straining in the Midst of the Storm

*"A furious squall, storm, came up, and the waves broke
over the boat, so that it was nearly swamped."*
Mark 4:37
Mark 4:35-41
Good People in Bad Places

Today we continue our series of sermons on ***Good People
in Bad Places***. The title of the message is **The Twelve Disciples:
Straining in the Midst of the Storm**.

In an earlier sermon we touched upon another storm as we
talked about **Simon Peter: Sinking in the Stormy Sea of Fear**.
This account is found in Mark 6, John 6 and Matthew 14. It is
interesting in that only Matthew records Peter walking on the
water in the context of this storm. Also, initially in that storm,
Jesus was not in the boat with the twelve disciples, but He was
watching from a mountainside. He then came down the mountain,
placed His feet upon the Sea of Galilee, and He walked on the
water to where they were. Peter saw Him, got out of the boat and
walked towards Jesus.

You may remember, in that sermon we said four things
about Peter sinking in the stormy sea of fear:
First, we talked about Simon Peter's **desire** as he said
"Lord, if You will permit me, let me get out of the boat and walk
with You on the water."
Secondly, we spoke of Peter's **decision** as he decided to
get out of the boat.
Thirdly, we spoke of Peter's **dilemma** as he took his eyes
off Jesus, looked at the wind, and he began to sink.
Fourthly, we spoke of Peter's **dependence** as Jesus
stretched out His hand, and Peter took it. Peter depended upon
Jesus as our Lord lifted him up.

Now while this storm is found later in the Gospels, our

text for the storm we are studying today is taken from Mark 4. In this instance, Jesus preached from a boat to the people who were on shore. I have never preached to people from a boat, but I have preached to people who were in boats. On the Sunday before Memorial Day, I preach at the Church in the Pines at Lake Martin near Dadeville, Alabama. The worship service is in a huge tabernacle next to the lake. On the Sunday of Memorial Day weekend, the tabernacle is packed and overflowing with people. Many have to sit outside the tabernacle on blankets and folding chairs. Also, there are people in boats on the lake who are close to the tabernacle within hearing distance. They worship in their boats, and they use their boats as pews; but in this instance, Jesus used a boat for a pulpit as He preached to them.

In His sermon, Jesus shared many wonderful parables and stories in Mark 4. He talked about The Parable of the Sower. He compared our lives to a candle, and He told about The Parable of the Mustard Seed. Then as evening came, the disciples got in the boat with Him, and they set out to cross the Sea of Galilee. While on the sea, they encountered a terrible storm; and as we sail across the waters of life, we are going to encounter terrible storms also.

There are three things I want us to note about the storm. I want us to note:

I.	**The Inclusiveness of It**	**(vs. 35-36)**
II.	**The Inevitability of It**	**(vs. 37)**
III.	**The Instruction of It**	**(vs. 38-39)**

I.   The Inclusiveness of It

In your mind, I want you to envision the disciples in that boat with our Lord. I believe all twelve of them were there. Verses 35 and 36 tell us the disciples were with Him in the boat. In your mind, I want you to see Matthew; Andrew; Thomas; Bartholomew; Philip; Thaddaeus; James, the son of Alphaeus; Simon the Zealot; Judas Iscariot; Simon Peter; John; and James, the son of Zebedee.

I believe all of the disciples were in the boat that encountered the storm. It included all of them, and it is important for us to note that the storm includes all of us in this sanctuary and those watching by television. The storm is inclusive of everybody. No one is immune from it. No one is exempt from it. The storm includes all of us.

II.   The Inevitability of It

Verse 37 simply says, "A storm arose." The NIV is more graphic as it says, "A furious (and it is interesting that the Greek word used for furious is the word μεγάλη, and this is a word that means large and huge. We've transliterated from this word our English term, mega.) squall, storm came up, and the waves broke over the boat, so that it was nearly swamped."

The thing I want us to notice under this second point is that the storm is inevitable. The storm is coming. It came to them, and it is going to come to us.

James 1:2 says, "Count it all joy when the troubles of life come." Notice, James does not say, "if they come," but "**when** they come." The storm is coming.

Proverbs 3:25 says, "Do not be afraid of fear or sudden desolation **when** it comes." Notice again, not if, but when. Did you notice the hymn we sang a moment ago? We didn't sing "if the storms of life are raging, stand by me," but we sang "**when** the storms of life are raging." Yes, the storm is going to come, and it can come in a raging way.

The storm is inevitable. It is coming. It may come slowly, deliberately and unobtrusively; or it may come, like it did in our text, suddenly, savage and swiftly, but it will come.

Yes, the storm is inevitable. Maybe some of you listening right now have recently passed through the storm. Perhaps some of you are in the midst of the storm at this very moment. For some of you, the storm is going to break in the future. But we need to understand that the storm is inevitable, and the storm is coming.

Mary Tyler Moore said, "none of us gets out of here without any pain," and while the storm can be painful, the storm **is** definitely inevitable.

III.   The Instruction of It

The storm can instruct us. The storm can teach us. There are **two** parts to this instruction packet found in our text:

First, we must do **our** part. Notice verse 38 tells of how the disciples called upon Him as they said, "Teacher, don't You care if we drown?"

Secondly, our Lord always does **His** part as verse 39 says, "He got up, rebuked the wind and said to the waves, 'Quite, peace! Be still!' Then the wind died down and it was completely calm."

If we are willing to learn, then God will teach us in the storm and about the storm. There are **three** important lessons we need to learn about the storm:

One, God does not send the storm.

Notice verse 37 again as it says, "The storm arose." No where in the text does it say that God sent the storm. I believe that storm was caused by conflicting climate conditions in that part of the Galilean Basin.

I have never believed that God sends pain, hurt and affliction upon His people. I know some theologies teach this, and this idea of God's retributive justice is an important part of their belief system. But I do not believe that God sends the storm. To be certain, God does allow it. God does permit it, but He does not send it.

Two, God is with us in the midst of the storm.

It doesn't matter what storm you are in right now, you need to understand that just as Jesus was in the boat with the disciples, so your Lord is in the midst of your storm with you.

A man's son was tragically killed in an automobile

accident. He came to the church, and he rushed into the pastor's study and cried out, "Where was God when my son was killed?"

The kind pastor got up, put his arms around the distraught man and said, "He was in the same place He was when His Son was killed. He was weeping, and His heart was breaking for you."

Dr. Fred Craddock taught preaching at the Candler School of Theology at Emory for many years. He told of meeting a minister who did not have any arms. He was born that way. This minister then told Fred how as a little boy his mother had to dress him. This was a daily routine. Then one day his mother took all of his clothes and piled them in the middle of the bedroom and said, "Today, you are going to dress yourself." The young fellow started to cry and kick and scream as he said, "But Mother, I can't dress myself. I never have, and I don't know how!" Then the mother simply turned and walked out of the room and left her son there with his clothes. He continued to scream and cry. Then the young lad realized that if he was going to get dressed, he would have to do it himself. He struggled for several hours, and finally he dressed himself. Fred said that the boy did not learn until later that the entire time his mother was in the next room crying her heart out.

And you need to understand that in the midst of your storm, as you are struggling and hurting, your Lord is next to you, hurting right along with you.

Three, God can calm any storm in your life.

When we call upon Him, He will make the angry waves of anxiety lay down. He will cause the turbulent winds of stress to become calm; and like our text, He will bring a peace to you, and He will enable you to truly say, "It is well with my soul."

In closing, I want you to bow your heads, open your hearts and allow the words of this hymn to minister to you, to calm your storm and bring peace to your heart:

When peace, like a river, attendeth my way,
When sorrows like sea billows roll;
Whatever my lot, Thou hast taught me to say,

It is well, it is Well with my soul.

Though Satan should buffet, though trials should
Come, let this blest assurance control, that Christ has
Regarded my helpless estate, and hath shed His own
Blood for my soul.

And, Lord, haste the day when my faith shall be sight,
The clouds be rolled back as a scroll; the trump shall
Resound, and the Lord shall descend, Even so, it is
Well with my soul.

It is well, it is well, with my soul, with my soul,
It is well, it is well with my soul.

Chapter 3

Jairus: Struggling with Grief in His Own Home
Mark 5:35-41
Good People in Bad Places

In this message today we are going to look at the **bad place** of grief. There are many biblical examples I could have chosen for this sermon.

In II Samuel 17, there is the account of the death of Absalom, a death that has been immortalized through poetry. As David looked upon his dying son, it tells us that he wept and cried from a heart filled with grief, "O Absalom, my son; Absalom, my son."

Or we could have chosen the Widow of Nain. We read about her story in Luke chapter 7, and it is a story filled with grief as she not only lost her husband, but her son died also.

Or we could have chosen Mary and Martha in John chapter 11. Their brother Lazarus died, and they cried, "Jesus, do You not care that our brother has died?" And then to exacerbate the dilemma and add to the grief even more, Jesus waited three days before He came to be with them.

Or another example could be Mary, the mother of Jesus, as she stood at the foot of the cross as her son was being crucified. You may remember that three years ago we did a series of seven sermons on "The Seven Last Words" over the Sundays in Lent. In the third sermon, we talked about the words that Jesus spoke to Mary at the foot of the cross. Jesus looked down upon her, and it is interesting that He did not call her mother, but rather He addressed her as woman. It is the Greek word *γυνή*, and in that sermon we pointed out that as Jesus was dying upon the cross, He was theologically doing two things: One, He was **consummating** our salvation. Two, He was forever **changing** His relationship with Mary. For in that moment He was becoming her Savior instead of her son. From that time on He would be the Savior of every person who has ever lived. Now, that is the theological explanation of it, but as Mary stood at the foot of the cross, watching her son die, I can tell you that she was not looking upon the death of her son theologically nearly as much as she was looking upon it maternally and with a grieving heart. Can you imagine, as a mother, standing, looking up and watching your own son die and feeling the very drops of his blood fall upon you? Oh, I think she experienced what the hymn writer later was to write about:

> *But drops of grief can ne'er repay*
> *The debt of love I owe.*

I can only imagine how her heart must have been filled and laden with grief as she watched her son die before her very eyes.

Yes, there are many excellent examples from which I could choose, but we are going to look at a man named Jairus whose story is found in Mark 5:35-42. As we have done in all of these sermons so far, there are two things I want you to notice about Jairus in this selection of Scripture.

One, He was a **good man**. Our text tells us that he was the ruler of the synagogue, and that was a position of honor and prestige.

But two, he found himself in a very **bad place** as his little twelve year old daughter had died.

Against the background of these verses found in Mark 5:35-42, there are four **thoughts** I want us to note and glean from these verses. I want us to note:

I. **The Untrue Thought**
    (That God does not care about my grief, vs. 35)
II. **The Unassuming Thought**
    (That I do not have to do anything about my grief, vs. 36)
III. **The Unique Thought**
    (That my grief can manifest itself in many ways, vs. 38-40)
IV. **The Ultimate Thought**
    (That God is in absolute control, vs. 41)

I.   The Untrue Thought
(That God does not care about my grief, vs. 35)

I want you to notice verse 35 as it says, "While Jesus was still speaking, some men came from the house of Jairus, the synagogue ruler. 'Your daughter is dead,' they said, 'Why bother the teacher anymore?'"

I want you to notice the question they asked: "Why bother the teacher anymore?" Another translation records them as saying, "Why trouble the Master anymore?"

Now the implication of that question is that Jesus was too busy to care about the death of his little girl. I mean after all, when you look at what He had already done in Mark chapter 5, it is obvious He was a very busy man. In the first part of chapter 5, He drove the demons out of Legion in the land of the Gadarenes. In the middle part of the chapter it tells of how He was mobbed by the multitudes as He healed a woman of a debilitating disease. Yes, He was very busy and those men were simply expressing their thoughts that Jesus was too busy to care about Jairus in this moment of his little girl's death.

And so often when we are grieving, we entertain that same untrue thought. We ask ourselves the questions, "How could God have time for me? How could He really care about me? He has a universe to look after. He has a world to run and take care of—and with all the mess and all the problems going on, that is a full time job. He has the sun, the moon and stars to keep in place. He is so busy. How could He care about me and my problems?"

Dear friend, nothing could be further from the truth. You need to understand that God cares about you. Jesus said in Matthew 10:29-31, "Are not two sparrows sold for a penny? Yet not one of them will fall to the ground apart from the will of your Father. And even the very hairs of your head are all numbered. So don't be afraid; you are worth more than many sparrows." And if God cares about a little bird who falls to the ground, then how much more does He care about you, O you of little faith?

The two most important facts you can know about God are: One, He loves you; and two, He cares about you.

I remember back in the year 2000, we went to the *Passion Play* in Oberammergau, Germany. It was a wonderful experience to be a part of that very special presentation. Following the *Passion Play*, several of us took an extended tour to Switzerland.

I remember our Swiss guide told us about a remote Swiss village, and in that village is one of the most beautiful churches in all of Switzerland. He said it is called "The Mountain Valley Cathedral." He told us that it has a high vaulted ceiling, high columns and magnificent stain glass windows. But the crown jewel of that church is the beautiful pipe organ. He told of how people would come from all over Switzerland and even Europe just to sit and hear the beautiful strains of that organ.

Then he said that one day they faced a huge problem. The high vaulted ceiling was still there. The huge columns were there. The magnificent stain glass windows were there, but an eerie silence pervaded the church because very little sound emanated from the organ. The only sounds that came forth were discordant and disharmonious. Something happened to the organ, and no longer could it be played effectively.

Experts came from all over Europe, and they tried to repair the organ, but all of their efforts were in vain.

One day an elderly old man who was very shabbily dressed appeared. He had in his hand a box of tools. He asked the custodian if he could go in and look at the organ. Very reluctantly he agreed.

The elderly man went into the sanctuary, closed the door and made his way to the organ. Using his set of tools, he began to disassemble the organ as he went deep into the interior of it. He worked for two days on the organ as he laboriously gave himself to the task of repairing it. And then on the third day at high noon, he took his place on the seat in front of the console. He lifted his hands high and then he came down upon the ivory keys—and the most beautiful music ever heard issued from the organ. The valley once again was filled with glorious music. Farmers dropped their plows, merchants closed their stores, students and teachers dropped their books and they all came to the church and sat in reverence and awe as they listened to the beautiful music.

After he finished, someone approached him and asked,

"How were you able to repair the organ when all of the other experts failed?"

The elderly man with misty eyes and a full throat and a trembling voice said, "You see, it was an inside problem. Fifty years ago I built, created and installed this organ right here. I know everything about this organ. I love it and I care about it." And then with a convicting voice he said, "Fifty years ago I **built** this organ, and now I have **restored** it."

You see, your grief can do one of two things in your life. It can psychologically ruin you, or it can spiritually restore you. Your grief is an inside job, and the very God who physically **created** you can spiritually **restore** you and use your grief to make you a better person.

Verse 35 tells us of how these men came to Jairus and said, "Why trouble the Master? Why bother the teacher?"

In your life, right now, maybe you are in the midst of grief, and you are wondering, does Jesus really care about me? Oh my friend, the Good News is He does care about you. He **created** you, and He wants to spiritually **restore** you through the grief process with His divine grace. You see, it is so easy for us to forget how much He cares, and we need to be reminded of His care.

II.   **The Unassuming Thought**
(That I do not have to do anything about my grief, vs. 36)

Look carefully at verse 36 as it says, "Do not be afraid; just believe."

God does His part by strengthening us and comforting us and caring for us, and we must do our part by believing. How do we believe? We believe by putting our trust and our faith in God, and then we get busy. James says, "Faith without works is dead." So we put our faith in God, and we work, and we stay busy. You see, grief can be helpful and therapeutic, but if you sit around your home and do nothing, it will imprison you and destroy you.

There are so many ways that you can activate your faith by staying busy. Get in a grief support group. It will affirm and strengthen you when you meet and share with Brothers and Sisters in Christ who share your experiences. Don't try to do it all by yourself. Volunteer and get busy in some church or civic function. Work in the Food Pantry. Go on a mission trip. Volunteer to visit shut-ins in our nursing homes. Do something constructive. Most importantly, notice what Jesus tells us to do in our text, verse 36, as He says, "Do not be afraid; just believe."

The Greek word that we translate just is *μόνον* as it means to be focused upon one thing. The word we translate believe is *πίστευε*. He says, "just believe." This Greek word we translate believe *πίστευε* is from the Greek derivative for faith, *πίστος*.

One of the other translations says, "Don't be afraid; **only believe**." I remember as a little boy growing up in the First Methodist Church in Opelika, there was a song that my father would lead our congregation in singing. The song was:

Only believe, Only believe;
All things are possible;
Only believe.

And, like Jairus, as we deal with the grief in our lives, we need to **believe**. We need to believe **three things**:

One, we need to believe, **personally**, that God is with us.

You need to believe that God is with you right now. You need to believe that you are never alone for your God is always by your side.

I officiate a lot of funerals, and in nearly every funeral I always read the 23rd Psalm. In Psalm 23:4, David says, "Yea though I walk through the valley of the shadow of death; I will not fear. For thou art with me."

In this verse we observe the juxtaposition of two powerful emotions: fear and faith. I want you to notice that David is sharing with us his answer to the question of fear. He states that he will not fear, and the reason he will not fear is because through faith he knows his God is by his side every step of the way.

You see, fear can descend and disturb your grief process more than any other emotion. Fear is the enemy of faith, and the one thing that conquers and defeats fear is faith.

Notice again that David tells us the reason he will not fear is because God is with him, and you eliminate the fear in your life by *only believing* that your God is with you and you are never alone.

Two, we need to believe, **spiritually**, that our loved ones in Christ who have died are in a sense still present with us right now. We need to believe this for three reasons.

First, we need to believe it because it is **attested** in Holy Scripture. The writer of Hebrews says in 12:1, "We are surrounded by a great cloud of witnesses." That means those loved ones in Christ who have died are in a **spiritual** sense surrounding us right now. The Bible teaches this important doctrine.

Secondly, we need to believe it because it is **affirmed** in the historic Creeds of the church. Earlier in the service we said, "I believe in the Communion of Saints." This is an important doctrine of our faith that was put into this creed by the church fathers. This statement, "I believe in the Communion of Saints," is just as much a part of our creedal system as is the first phrase, "I believe in God the Father Almighty." You believe it because the historic creeds of the church affirm it.

Thirdly, we need to believe it because it is **articulated** in the majestic Hymnody of the church. A few moments ago we sang:

> *Yet she on earth hath union*
> *With God the Three in One,*
> *And mystic sweet communion*
> *With those whose rest is won.*
> *O happy ones and holy!*
> *Lord, give us grace that we,*
> *Like them, the meek and lowly,*
> *On High may dwell with thee.*

One of the great ministers in Christendom was Dr. Norman Vincent Peale. In the middle part of the last century he was pastor of the great Marble Collegiate Church in New York City. At that time it was perhaps the leading church in Protestantism. Dr. Peale was an eloquent preacher. He was also a prolific writer. He wrote the book, **The Power of Positive Thinking**, and he became the editor of *Guidepost* magazine.

In a *Guidepost* article, Dr. Peale tells of how many years ago he was preaching at the Georgia Annual Conference. He describes it in *Guidepost* like this:

And just last year, when I was preaching at a Methodist gathering in Georgia, I had the most startling experience of all. At the end of the final session, the presiding Bishop asked all the ministers in the audience to come forward, form a choir and sing an old, familiar hymn. I was sitting on the speakers' platform, watching them come down the aisles. And suddenly, among them, I saw my father. I saw him as plainly as I ever saw him when he was alive. He seemed about forty, vital and handsome. He was singing with the others. When he smiled at me, and put up his hand in the old familiar gesture, for several unforgettable seconds it was as if my father and I were alone in that big auditorium. Then he was gone, but in my heart the certainty of his presence was indisputable. He was there, and I know that someday, somewhere. I'll meet him again.

Dr. Peale, felt that was God's way of reminding him of this important doctrine of our faith, "The Communion of the Saints," and it was God's way of reminding him that in a **spiritual**

25

sense his father was still with him.

One of the most Christ like people I've ever known was Rev. Cy Dawsey. Brother Dawsey was a retired minister who was in our church here for several years. He and his wife, Marshlea, had been missionaries to Brazil. I greatly admired and respected Cy Dawsey. One of the reasons I loved him so much was because he reminded me so much of my father. Yes, they shared the same first name, but even more they shared a deep devotion to Jesus Christ, and in Brother Dawsey I could see the spirit of Jesus. He meant so much to me.

I remember after my father died, many times I would call Brother Dawsey. Nobody was ever aware of this but Cy Dawsey and me. When I was facing a situation in the church, or I had a big decision to make, or when my soul was troubled about something, I would call him and talk to him at length. Many times we would meet in our sanctuary, and he would pray for me. I found such strength and inspiration in this Godly man. He died several years ago.

Brother Dawsey loved to help me serve Holy Communion. That was one of the great joys of his retirement years. I remember how much it meant to me to have him stand by my side as we served the Blessed Sacrament together. I would go first and serve the bread. He would follow and serve the cup, and he would always say, "The blood of our Lord Jesus that was shed for the remission of our sins."

I remember it as though it were yesterday. It was two years ago on World Wide Communion Sunday, and it was one of those special services where the air was thick with the presence of God. I could feel God's love and grace as I preached, and especially as I was serving Holy Communion. I never will forget how I felt the presence of Cy

Dawsey right next to me. It was so real that I felt I could have reached out and touched him. I remember how emotional that experience was for me as I had tears in my eyes. And then I clearly and audibly heard Cy say these words as he was serving the cup, "The blood of our Lord Jesus that was shed for the remission of our sins." I could feel his presence, and I heard his voice, and I looked and he was gone.

Like Dr. Norman Vincent Peale, I believe that was God's way of reminding me again of this precious doctrine of "The Communion of Saints," and it was God's way of reminding me that my loved ones in a **spiritual** sense are still present here with me.

Three, we need to believe, **eternally**, that our loved ones in Christ who have died will live forever. Do you remember several years ago we did a series of sermons on "The Seven Great I Am Affirmations of Jesus." Those seven affirmations are found in the Book of John. We began with "I Am the Bread of Life," "I Am the Light of the World," and we concluded with the affirmations "I Am the Way, the Truth and the Life," and "I Am the True Vine." The fifth "*I Am*" affirmation is a statement of Jesus when He said, "*I Am the Resurrection and the Life*." As you deal with the grief in your life and think about your loved one in Christ, you believe our Lord when He said, "I am the Resurrection and the Life," and you believe that those who trust in Christ will never die, but they will live forever.

One of the most moving services in our church each year is on All Saints' Day. It is usually the last Sunday of October or the first Sunday in November, and that is the Sunday that we remember our loved ones in Christ who have died and moved into the nearer presence of the Heavenly Father. We show the faces of these loved ones on the screens in our sanctuary, and they are smiling down as they look at us. It is especially touching to me because I've conducted most of their funeral services, and I have been with their families during their time of grief. It is a very moving service.

We have a similar service when our Annual Conference meets in June. On Monday morning we have a Memorial Service when we remember the ministers and wives who died over the past year. That is a very inspiring service. I've sat, and I've reflected, and I've looked into the faces of some of the dear ministers who have served this church, ministers like Joel McDavid and Charles Britt, who have made heaven all the more lovelier with their presence. That is the most inspiring time of Annual Conference for me.

At the 2012 Annual Conference, I will be preaching the Memorial Service sermon. The Annual Conference has invited me to be their preacher for that special service. It is always an inspiring and moving service, and it is certainly a great honor. But with that honor is an awesome responsibility as I seek to speak words that will bring comfort and hope to the grieving families of those ministers who have outrun us to the Father's House. Please pray that God will use me to bring comfort and strength and inspiration to them.

As we conclude the second point, I want you to close your eyes for a moment. I want you to think of some loved one in Christ in your family who has died or some dear one in Christ for whom you are grieving. Like those screens in our church, and at Annual Conference, you vividly see that smiling face before you. The Bible says in the Book of John, "the Holy Spirit will bring these things to your remembrance." You ask God through the Spirit to place that picture before you now. And as you think about that dear person in Christ, you remind yourself of your belief that Jesus is the Resurrection and the Life, and those who believe in Him will never die. They will live forever. Hallelujah!

III.   The Unique Thought
        (That my grief can manifest itself in many ways, vs. 38)

Verse 38 says, "When they came to the home of the

synagogue ruler, Jesus saw a commotion, with people crying and wailing loudly." Notice the word "commotion." It is the Greek word *θόρυβον*, and one Greek scholar tells us it is a word that means "utter emotional consternation." It is a word filled with great emotion.

Over my years in the ministry I have conducted many funerals and I have been with many people in grief stricken and traumatic situations, and I have found that people respond differently to crisis situations, and the reason is because we all are psychologically, emotionally, mentally and spiritually constituted differently—and thus we respond with different feelings to various situations.

There is an excellent article on emotional response in the March 4 issue of *Newsweek*. It is adapted from a book, **The Emotional Response of the Brain**, by Richard Davidson, who teaches Psychology at the University of Wisconsin. It develops the thesis that there are six key elements of emotional style. They are: One, Resilience; two, Outlook; three, Self-Awareness; four, Social Intuition; five, Attention; six, Sensitivity to Context.

And the article begins with this paragraph:

> *If you believe most pop psychology, you probably assume that most of us react to life events in just about the same way—there is a grieving process, a sequence of events when we fell in love, a standard response to be jilted.*
>
> *But these one-size-fits-all assumptions are not true. In decades of research into the neurobiology of emotion, I've seen thousands of people who share similar backgrounds respond in dramatically different ways to the same experience. Why does one person recover quickly from divorce while another remains mired in self-recrimination or despair? Why does one sibling bounce back from a job loss while another feels worthless for years? And*

why can one father shrug off the botched call of a Little League umpire who called his daughter out while another leaps out of his seat and screams at the ump until his face turns purple? The answer that has emerged from my research is that these differences reflect what I call Emotional Style-a constellation of reactions and coping responses that differ in kind, intensity and duration. Just as each person has a unique fingerprint and unique face, each of us has a unique emotional profile.

I've observed that people can respond differently to the very same situation. Some people are very analytical in their response. Others are very cerebral, and this is especially true in a university setting. Some are stoic in their response. Some are emotionally subdued while others are, like the people in our text in verse 38, emotionally demonstrative. But one thing I have observed is that in nearly every instance there are nearly always tears. Many times they are quiet and seemingly silent tears—but there are tears.

Yes, there are many different emotional responses in the process that we call grief.

Another interesting emotion is found in verse 40, and that is the emotion of laughter. I want you to notice that verse 40 says, "But they laughed at him." The Greek verb we translate laughed is *κατεγέλων*, and this emotion of laughter must certainly be understood within its proper context. Jesus had just made the statement, "Your little girl is not dead. She is only sleeping." The response of the people was that of laughter, and to be sure, it was a laughter of scorn and skepticism and cynicism, but still it reminds us of the powerful emotion of laughter.

It is interesting that in my in-depth study for this series of sermons on the subject of grief, I have found very little reference to the emotion of laughter. I've not found it in any grief books that I have studied, and I have not even found it in many of the grief stricken situations in Holy Scripture.

In II Samuel 18 when David was grieving the death of his son Absalom, it tells us that David wept. Nowhere is there the mention of laughter.

In Luke chapter 7, there is the grief filled story of the Widow of Nain whose only son died. This particular chapter is a study in grief. It speaks of how they wept, but nowhere is the emotion of laughter mentioned.

And then in John chapter 11, as Mary and Martha were mourning the death of their brother Lazarus, it tells us how they wept. It even says in verse 35 that "Jesus wept," but nowhere in this narrative is there the mention of laughter, and the reason is because we do not normally associate laughter with grief; but it is my belief that laughter and a happy heart can be very helpful and therapeutic.

Proverbs 17:22 says, "A cheerful heart is a good medicine, but a crushed spirit dries up the bones."

Quite often if someone is grieving the death of a loved one, a caring doctor will prescribe medicine to help that person get through that immediate and initial grief process, but I want you to notice that the writer of Proverbs tells us that a happy and smiling heart can be just as effective as medicine, for it says, "A cheerful heart is a good medicine."

A magazine that I enjoy reading each week is *The Economist*. Somebody gives me a free copy every week. I am very economical with *The Economist*. It does not cost anything.

In *The Economist*, I read that the Recession started with what they call the Bear Market in March of 2007, and that ushered in what we know as "The Great Recession." Some may question the date of the start of "The Great Recession," but we all know the "The Great Depression" started with the crash of the stock market in October of 1929.

American historians tell us that Will Rogers, as much as anybody, helped America learn to laugh its way through the Great Depression.

During that time Will Rogers said, "Many look at the plight of the people, and they asked me if I pray for the Congress. I tell them, 'No, I look at the plight of Congress, and I pray for the people.'" The Congress of that day probably thought that was about as funny as you did today, but Will Rogers showed America the therapeutic value of laughter and how it can help us. Laughter and a smiling heart are so very important.

One of the funniest people whom I've ever known was Bob Baggott. Bob was pastor for many years at the First Baptist Church in Opelika, and in retirement he pastored the Farmville Baptist Church in our community. He was one of the most beloved ministers in the state of Alabama. He served for many years as the Chaplain for the Auburn University football team. Bob was a dear friend of mine.

Bob was a student in engineering at Georgia Tech, and he said God called him to preach one morning in class while he was struggling with and taking a calculus exam.

Bob also served the First Baptist Church in Birmingham, and when he was the pastor there he told of receiving a call from one of the funeral directors in that city. The director asked if he could conduct a funeral for a lady who did not have a pastor. Bob readily obliged, and he went to the funeral home, met briefly with the family and prepared to do the funeral.

He knew very little about the woman. The only thing he knew was that she was a dedicated Christian, and the only reason he was doing the funeral was because they simply needed a pastor, any pastor, and Bob was the only one they could find.

Bob got into his funeral message, and all of a sudden he realized he could not remember the woman's name. He had never met her, and he knew very little about her. The only thing he knew was that she was a dedicated Christian woman.

He then got an inspiration as he stopped right in the middle of his sermon and said to that small crowd of people: "One of the greatest gestures of affirmation and celebration, and one of the greatest tributes we can make to our dear departed sister in Christ is for all of us in unison to call her name. I want all of us to shout out her name at the count of three. Bob then counted, "one, two, three–and they all shouted at the top of their voices, *Susie!*"

Then Bob looked up to heaven and shouted, "God bless

you *Susie*, as you are looking down from heaven, we are remembering you!" Yes, a smiling and laughing heart can help assuage the pain of a grieving heart.

I read about two professional public speakers who were discussing their careers. One said to the other, "What is the most difficult speech you have ever had to give?" The other public speaker immediately replied, "I was invited to address a Convention of Undertakers and Funeral Directors in Las Vegas. I had to speak on the subject 'How to look sad at a $20,000 funeral!'"

Now, for not anything in the world would I negate the seriousness and solemnity of the grieving process, but my dear friends, there are some things that we had better learn to laugh with and smile at or else we will weep and be crushed beneath the emotional load of it.

I believe that within all of us there is an innate desire to be happy and positive in our grief. I've conducted many funerals, and I have never had a person tell me that they wanted the funeral to be sad and despondent. They always say, "We want the service for our loved one to be celebrative, positive, happy and upbeat!"

Several years ago I wrote a book entitled *Healing Thoughts...To Mend Hurting Hearts*. I based the book upon the words of Jesus in Luke 4 when our Lord said, "The Spirit of the Lord is upon Me...for He has sent Me to heal the brokenhearted."

I sent a copy of this book to every family within our church who was grieving the loss of a loved one with the prayer that it would help mend their hurting hearts.

In this book I talk about the healing power of Jesus. I point out how He is able to heal us physically as He still touches bodies, and I point out five ways that Jesus brings physical healing. I also point out how He heals relationally. He heals marriages, homes and families. He especially, when it seems that all hope is gone, heals relationships between estranged friends.

I write of how He heals damaged emotions. I have a chapter in the book entitled *The Healing of Bad Memories*. That is a sermon that I preached here several years ago. Actually the entire book is a compilation of sermons that I did here at AUMC. The inspiration for the chapter on *The Healing of Bad Memories* came from a dear friend who was a member of my church at Kingswood in Mobile, Alabama. His name was Dr. Ben Ringsdorf. Ben was one of the closest friends that I have ever had. He was one of the sweetest and kindest and gentlest persons I've ever known. I officiated at his wedding and our friendship grew over the years.

Ben was a fighter pilot in Vietnam, and he was shot down. He ejected from the plane and upon landing, the first people he saw were the people whose village he had just bombed. You can imagine the anger they expressed towards him. Ben shared with me what they did to him. He then served as a POW in Vietnam for several years. Ben told me of some the awful things he experienced. I am not sure he ever revealed some of those experiences to anybody else.

Upon his release, Ben came back, went to the University of South Alabama Medical School and graduated with honors. He then opened a medical practice in Mobile.

Ben graphically shared with me some of his experiences in that Vietcong prison and how those bad memories still had the power and capability to continually haunt him every day. As he spoke, many times in the midst of his tears, he would emotionally breakdown, and I would put my arms around him, and we would kneel and pray together.

I never will forget one of the last things Ben said to me. I remember he had difficulty speaking because he shared with me that his throat had been crushed by the butt of a rifle. He said to me, "Brother George, as a physician, I want to help people get well physically, but as my pastor, I want you to help me and other people get well emotionally and find healing from our bad memories of the past. People have more bad memories from the past then you can possibly imagine."

I have another chapter in that book on *grief*, and in that chapter I reference the book of Dr. Kathryn Kubler-Ross, and I discuss her five emotional stages of grief. I list each one, comment upon it, and then make a theological response to it. I'm sure you are familiar with them, and in nearly every grief situation we all go through these stages. Some last longer than others, but usually we can find ourselves in one of these five stages. The real tragedy is there are some stages out of which people never emerge, and they become imprisoned. As I share them, you can perhaps think of some grieving person who is incarcerated in one of these cells of grief and cannot break free.

There is the stage of **shock**. When something bad happens, our initial reaction is that of *shock*. Two, there is the stage of **denial**. We psychologically deny what has happened. Thirdly, there is the stage of **anger**. We become angry. We become angry sometimes at other people involved in the situation. We even become angry with ourselves, and many times people become angry with God. The fourth stage is the stage of **depression**. We go through a period of depression where we don't want to do anything. Sometimes we withdraw from society. And then finally, there is the stage of **acceptance** when we begin to accept the situation.

In this book I add a sixth stage, and that is the stage of **resolution**, as we must resolve to pick ourselves up and get on with our lives.

But if I were writing that book today, I would add a seventh stage and the seventh stage would be—**Learn to smile through the tears, and learn to laugh**. Yes, learn again how to laugh. It is so important to understand the words of the Proverb: "A merry and laughing heart does good like a medicine," and when we are grieving the death of a loved one in Christ, we have every right to be happy and glad and joyful because that loved one is safe in the arms of Jesus.

We can say along with Paul in I Corinthians 15:55, "O death where is your sting? O grave, where is your victory?" Thanks, (the Greek word we translate thanks here is the word χάρα. In the English, it is *chara*, and from that Greek root we get words like *charisma* and *charismatic*. What is interesting is that usually in the Greek New Testament the word "thanks" or "thank you" is taken from the word ευχαριστος, the word from which we get our term Eucharist as in Holy Eucharist. It means the "meal of thanksgiving," as the word Eucharist means to give thanks. But what is interesting is that the word used here is not ευχαριστος, but it is the word χάρα. It is a word that not only **means to be thankful**, but at the **same time** it means to be **very joyful**. The deeper meaning of this word is **joy**. For example, in Philippians 4:4 Paul says, "*Rejoice* in the Lord always and again I say unto you **rejoice**." The Greek word that we translate as **rejoice** is found two times in this verse. It is the word χάρα, the same word that is used in I Corinthians 15:55. And so Paul is telling us not only to be **thankful**, but to be thankful in a **joyful** and **happy** way.) "Thanks be to God who gives to us the victory through the Lord Jesus Christ."

Our text in verses 38-40 speaks, of several emotions, but the note that I especially want to conclude this point with is the high note of **Joy**.

IV.   The Ultimate Thought
         (That God is in absolute control, vs. 41)

Our text for this fourth *thought* is taken from verse 41 as it says, "He took her by the hand and said to her, '*Talitha koum!*' (Which means, 'Little girl, I say to you, get up!') Immediately the girl stood up and walked around (she was twelve years old). At this they were completely astonished."

It is important for us to understand that the New Testament was written in Greek, but Jesus spoke Aramaic. In the Bible, in the book of Mark, there are several Aramaisms of Jesus. In Mark 7:34, Jesus was ministering to a man who could not speak nor hear, and he said, "**ephatha**" which is an Aramaic word that means "Be opened." And then in Mark 14:36, Jesus was praying in the Garden of Gethsemane and he prayed "*Abba* Father." The terms "**Ephphatha**" and "**Abba**" are Aramaic words.

And in our text for today we find another Aramaism as Jesus says, "*Talitha koum!*" Dr. William Barclay in his *Commentary on Mark*, gives an interesting word of explanation about this phrase found in Mark 5:41. He writes:

There is one lovely thing here. 'Talitha koum!' is Aramaic for 'Maid arise.' How did this little bit of Aramaic get itself imbedded in the Greek of the Gospels? There can be only one reason. Mark got his information from Peter, and Peter was there. He was one of the chosen three, the inner circle that saw it happen. And he could never forget the voice of Jesus. In his mind and memory he could hear that 'Talitha koum!' all his life. The love, the gentleness, the caress of it lingered with him forever, so much that he was unable to think of it in Greek at all because he could only hear it in his memory, in the voice of Jesus and the very words that Jesus spoke.

For just a moment I want you to use your imagination in a very vivid way. I want you to see Jesus as He went into the room of that little girl. He stood by her bed, looked at her and spoke in the beautiful Aramaic language saying, "*Talitha koum*" which means "Little girl, I say to you, stand up." It is my belief that right then and there that little girl opened her eyes and looked around. I believe she rubbed her eyes with her knuckles, and a faint smile creased her mouth. I believe she then looked around the room and saw her dear mother. And then I believe her eyes focused upon Peter, James and John, three strange men whom she had probably never seen before. And then I believe she looked upon the Lord Jesus standing there in His resplendent glory. And then I believe she looked over and saw her dad, and the Bible tells us that immediately she sat up. She then stood up, and I believe her eyes began to sparkle and a big smile came across her lips.

Fathers have a very special and unique relationship with their little girls. I know. Now keep in mind, it was the faith of her father that became the catalyst for this miracle, for verse 36 tells of how Jesus said specifically to Jairus, "Only believe," and it was because of the belief and faith of Jairus that this miracle came to fruition.

I believe this little girl walked over to her father.

I believe she put her arms around his waist and said,

"Daddy, where have you been? I have missed you so much. Please don't ever leave me."

I remember when we lived in Mobile and our daughter, Mallory, was a little girl. She was about seven years of age. One Sunday afternoon she was riding her bicycle, and she hit a curb, and she was thrown over the top of her bicycle and hurt her mouth. Her bottom lip was severely cut. I remember how she left her bicycle and came running home. I'll never forget how her little Sunday dress was covered with blood and she was crying. My wife and I immediately rushed her to the doctor.

I remember the nurse came out to get Mallory, and I will never forget the way Mallory looked up at me and said, "Daddy, please don't leave me. Please stay with me."

I took my little girl's hand and I went into the doctor's office with her, and I sat by her side while he sewed up her bottom lip. There are three things I distinctly remember about that experience.

One, she quit crying. Two, she held my hand tightly through the whole procedure, and I held her hand tightly. And, three, she never took her eyes off me while he was sewing her lip. I never took my eyes off her. I held her hand and looked at her, and she felt calm and secure.

I wonder if right now in the midst of your grief, there are tears in your eyes. Well, it so important for you to know that He, your Heavenly Father, can wipe away those tears, and it's even more important to know that He is right there by your side, and He longs to hold your hand. Also, as Psalm 32:8 says, "He wants to guide you with His eyes," and He longs to feel that closeness to you at this very moment.

This is one of the most beautiful and miraculous stories in all of Holy Scripture, and we rejoice at the power and Lordship of Jesus over life, emotion and even death.

In closing, I want to say that I've known people and it did not happen like it did in this scriptural account. They brought their little child to Jesus, and their little child did not come back. I very clearly remember one particular instance like that in our church family here at AUMC. Now I want you to listen very carefully to what I am going to say because it can help you.

In this scriptural instance, Jesus showed compassion on the parents. To bring that little girl back was a sad retrogression. It meant bringing her back to a world of fear, a world of problems and a world of sin. It meant that she would even have to go through the agony of death and dying again.

But in the other instance that is perhaps on your mind, our Lord showed compassion on the child.

Do you remember when Jesus took little children into His arms and loved them and cared for them. The middle stained glass window in our sanctuary is a depiction of Jesus loving the little children.

Now, if Jesus could love little children so much in an imperfect world like this, how much more does He love them in His perfect heaven? How much more does He love them in a perfect heaven, a place that is described in Revelation 21:4 as a place where the Bible says, "There will be no more pain, there will be no more sorrow, there will be no more tears, and there will be no more death," and most importantly, a place where "we shall see Jesus." How much more does He love them in that perfect place of heaven that the theologians call "An eternal oneness with God," and the hymn writer describes as "The Sweet Forever?"

The point is—whether they go or whether they stay, in the midst of your grief, you trust Jesus to do what is right, because in His love and mercy and grace and all encompassing compassion, and in His omnipotent power, you rest your faith upon the promise that "He doeth all things well."

I want us to think and sing about the loving power of our Lord:

All hail the power of Jesus' name!
Let angels prostrate fall,

39

Bring forth the royal diadem,
And crown him Lord of all.
Bring forth the royal diadem,
And crown him Lord of all.

Ye chosen seed of Israel's race,
Ye ransomed from the fall,
Hail him who saves you by his grace,
And crown him Lord of all.
Hail him who saves you by his grace,
And crown him Lord of all.

O that with yonder sacred throng,
We at his feet may fall!
We'll join the everlasting song,
And crown him Lord of all.
We'll join the everlasting song,
And crown him Lord of all.

Chapter 4

Martha: Stressing Out in the Kitchen of Worry
*"'Martha, Martha,' the Lord answered, 'You are worried
and stressed out and upset (μεριμνᾶς καὶ θορυβάζῃ)
about many things (πολλά)...'"*
Luke 10:41
Luke 10:38-42
Good People in Bad Places

This is the next sermon in our series of messages on
Good People in Bad Places. In this sermon I want us to look at
Martha, and the title of the message is **Martha: Stressing Out in
the Kitchen of Worry**.

As we have done in other sermons in this series, let me
set the background for this selection of Scripture.

Our text immediately follows The Parable of the Good
Samaritan. Many say this particular parable is the most famous
parable Jesus ever told. There are others who feel that The
Parable of the Prodigal Son is the most famous. Abraham
Lincoln said, "The Parable of the Prodigal Son is the greatest
short story ever told." The forefathers and foremothers of our
church must have felt The Parable of the Good Samaritan was
the greatest parable because it is the only parable that is depicted
in our stain glass windows.

After sharing this beautiful parable, I believe Jesus was
very tired. I don't know of anything in the ministry that can be
more exhausting than preaching and teaching, especially when it
is done with passion and conviction—and Jesus always preached
and taught with passion and conviction.

I know that for me, nothing tires me out anymore than
preaching, but I feel like Bishop Frances Asbury, the first Bishop
of North American Methodism, when he said, "Sometimes I get
tired **in** the work, but I never get tired **of** the work."

But sometimes when we are tired, we find relaxation and

refreshment by going to a place where we feel affirmed and loved. I believe Jesus found this place in the home of Martha and Mary.

Notice that verse 38 of our text tells us that Jesus "came to a village where a woman named Martha opened her home to Him."

In this message, there are four things that I want us to notice about Martha as they are revealed in the verses in our text. I want us to notice that she was:

I.	**A Wonderful Woman**	**(vs. 39)**
II.	**A Worried Woman**	**(vs. 40)**
III.	**A Wounded Woman**	**(vs. 41)**
IV.	**A Wise Woman**	**(vs. 42)**

I.   A Wonderful Woman

Now I use the word "wonderful" in a spiritually and a scripturally applicable way.

You remember when Isaiah prophesied the coming of Jesus, he said, "His name will be called Wonderful, Counselor, Mighty God, Everlasting Father, Prince of Peace," but notice first of all, Isaiah said His Name shall be called "Wonderful."

And Martha was a wonderful woman.

Verse 39 says that her sister Mary, "sat at the Lord's feet listening to what He said," and I believe Martha, along with her sister Mary, listened to what Jesus was saying. What a wonderful thing for these two sisters to do.

In this series of sermons we have talked about many people, but the thing I want you to notice about each one of them is how wonderful they were.

Elijah preached that powerful sermon on Mount Carmel. How wonderful!

David was described as "the man after God's own heart." How wonderful!

Jesus said of John the Baptist, "There has never been a greater man born of woman than John." How wonderful!

Paul described Euodia and Syntyche as his "co-laborers in the Gospel." How wonderful!

Aside from Peter, James and John were closer to Jesus than any of the other disciples. How wonderful!

In our last message we talked about Simon Peter and how he was **Sinking in the Stormy Sea of Fear**, but you remember after that, Jesus said to Simon Peter, "You are Peter, and upon this rock I will build my church, and the gates of hell shall not prevail against it." How wonderful!

The thing that I want you to notice about all of these men and women is how wonderful they were. And the thing I want you to understand about yourself is how wonderful you are. You are a wonderful person!

Just turn to the person next to you and say, "You are wonderful!"

In one of the other services, I had a lady say to me, "Dr. Mathison, when you told us to turn and say to the person sitting next to us, 'you are wonderful,' I sure the heck didn't want to say it to my husband because we had had an argument that morning before church. But when I told him he was wonderful, he smiled at me and took my hand, and I felt good all through the rest of the service." But he is wonderful, and she is wonderful, and all of the people we have studied in this series were wonderful—and you are especially a wonderful person.

But although you are wonderful, like all of these others, there are times when you will find yourself in *a bad place*.

II.   A Worried Woman

I remember several years ago there was a popular song by the Kingston Trio entitled *It Takes a Worried Man to Sing a Worried Song*. Martha was a worried woman, and I believe she was singing a worried song.

Verse 40 says, "But Mary was <u>distracted</u> by all the

preparations that had to be made."

The Greek word we translate as <u>distracted</u> is the word ***peristatto***, and it is the combination of two words in the Greek. It is the word peri, which means to encircle or surround, and from that Greek root we get words like periscope and perimeter. The word ***peristatto*** means to be bound or encumbered by something. The King James Version renders the word to say, "She was cumbered..." so when it says she was distracted by the preparation, it simply means that she was anxious and worried and all stressed out, and I don't know of anything that can stress you out anymore than having somebody important in your home for dinner.

I read about a young minister who had just graduated from Seminary. His wife and he and their little boy were serving a small church. He invited his District Superintendent to preach for him, and following the service they had the District Superintendent and his wife in their parsonage for Sunday dinner.

The parsonage was located next door to the church, and following the service they invited the District Superintendent and his wife into their home.

Before the District Superintendent got there, the minister's wife said to their five year old son, "Johnny, the District Superintendent is your daddy's boss. He is a wonderful man, but there is something I must tell you. He is a handsome man, but he has a very large nose. He is very sensitive about his nose, so when he comes don't you stare at it and don't you say a word about it!" The pastoral family sat down with the Superintendent for Sunday dinner, and little Johnny was staring at the District Superintendent's nose. The minister's wife kicked her little boy under the table and with a big smile, she very indiscreetly shook her head back and forth to the side. Then she picked up the fried chicken, looked at the District Superintendent and said, "Brother Smith, may I place a piece of fried chicken on your **nose**."

You see, there is something about any high office that can bring an element of stress. For example, if you are in the army, it would be like having the Five Star General to eat in your home. If you teach in the University, it would be like having the

President of the University for Sunday dinner, or if you work for a corporation like General Electric, it would be like having the CEO in your home.

I can understand why Martha was stressed out. Just think, for dinner she did not have the Bishop or District Superintendent or even the Pope; but she had somebody far more important than any of those people. She had Jesus there for dinner, and I can understand why she was "distracted in her preparation."

You see, the problem with stress is, it can reach a breaking point. It can cause you to do things that you do not mean to do. It can cause you to say things that you do not mean to say.

Just think of the last time you were under stress, and do you remember what you said? My wife tells me that sometimes when I get under stress, I can get a little snippy. I am not sure what that means, but I don't think it is good. I bet many of you get a little snippy also. That is what stress does to us.

Now notice what Martha, under stress, said in the last part of verse 40. She said, "Lord, don't you care that my sister has left me to do the work by myself? Tell her to help me!" You can feel the stress in this statement. Notice that she is ordering Jesus by telling Him what to do. "Tell her to help me!"

Friend, you don't tell Jesus what to do. You ask Him. Jesus said, in the Sermon on the Mount in Matthew 7:7-8, "Knock and it will be opened unto you. Seek and you will find. Ask and you shall receive." You see, Jesus does not instruct us to tell Him what to do, but we are to ask Him. But that is an example of the power of stress in an individual's life. It can cause you to say things that you don't mean to say—and perhaps later regret.

And so, Martha was a wonderful and good woman in the **bad place** of worry and stress.

III.   A Wounded Woman

Now Jesus knew exactly where Martha was hurting. Notice that Jesus said in verse 41, "Martha, Martha, you are worried and upset about many things." Yes, Jesus knew exactly where Martha was hurting, and my dear friend, right now your Lord knows where you are hurting and where you are wounded.

I mentioned earlier that this Scripture selection immediately follows The Parable of the Good Samaritan. In the preceding verses, Jesus tells of how a man was traveling from Jerusalem to Jericho. He was accosted by thieves, beaten, robbed, and he was left by the roadside wounded. Now this poor man was wounded physically. Jesus tells of how the Good Samaritan came and cared for him and poured medication into his wounds. It is a terrible thing to hurt physically.

Every week I go to the hospital, and I am in the presence of someone who is hurting physically. Physical pain is very hard to bear.

This week on the cover of *People* magazine is the picture of J.R. Martinez. He won the hearts of millions on the TV program, "Dancing with the Stars." J.R. was severely wounded in Iraq. He was flown back to the U.S., and during his recovery he said, "Every morning I was in the shower screaming and yelling. They would have to hold me down. There is no amount of medicine they can give to you that can take that pain away."

Yes, physical pain is awful.

But nearly every day I am in the presence of someone who is wounded and hurting spiritually and emotionally and mentally—and sometimes I think that can be even worse.

I wonder how many wounded and hurting people are in this service today?

And so, Martha was not only a wonderful woman and a worried woman, but she was also a wounded woman.

IV.   A Wise Woman

Look at verse 42, as the text goes on to say, and these are the words of Jesus speaking to her as He says, "But only one thing is needed. Mary has chosen what is better, and it will not be taken away from her."

I remember the first time I read verse 42, I had difficulty understanding what Jesus meant when He said, "Mary has chosen what is better, and it will not be taken away from her."

William Barclay in his **Commentary on the Book of Luke** helped me understand this as he points out that there in the home that day both of them were preparing a meal for Jesus. Martha was preparing an elaborate meal with several courses while Mary was preparing a simple one course meal. At that particular time, Jesus could see the Old Rugged Cross on the horizon. He had a lot on His mind, and rather than a complicated meal, He wanted something simple, and Mary prepared something very simple for Him.

And that is why Jesus said, "Only one thing is needed."

Now, the reason that I say Martha was wise is because she heeded this advice of Jesus. The next time we see Martha is in John 11:20. The brother of Mary and Martha had died and John 11:20 tells us that as soon as she heard that Jesus was coming, Martha went out to meet Him. In my mind I can see Martha as she was calm and collected and courageous with a positive attitude going out to meet her Lord. Mary was back at the house, but Martha was single mindedly focused upon seeing Him and being with Him.

And my dear friends, the most important thing you can do in addressing the stress in your life is to follow this wise admonition of Jesus, "*Only one thing is needed.*"

Only one thing is needed. You learn to live life just **one day** at a time. Don't worry about yesterday, and don't fret about tomorrow. Today is all you have. You live this one day. I was visiting a friend in the hospital who was very ill and he said to me, "Brother George, this illness has impressed upon me the fact that I have only one day at a time, and I am determined to live each day to its fullest." And you, dear friend, you just live in this day.

As you live this one day, you take it *one step* at a time. Don't get all bunched up and try to do too many things. You just take it one step at a time. When you came to church this morning and stood on the sidewalk in front of the porch, you didn't jump from the sidewalk to the porch, but you walked up the steps, taking it one step at a time. You do the same thing as you go through this day taking it one simple step at a time.

And then you just do *one thing* at a time. Paul wrote to the Philippians and said in chapter 3, "This one thing I do..." This past week I was in my study preparing sermons for Advent and the New Year. I was going through the Bible trying to find men and woman in the Old and New Testament who dealt with many of the same problems that we deal with today. I got to thinking of all the sermons that I must prepare. I started to feel stressed, and then the Holy Spirit spoke to me and said, "George, don't be stressed out about this. Don't you worry about it. You just do it *one sermon* at the time—and what a peace that brought to my mind."

Notice again that Jesus said to Martha in the midst of her stress, "*Only one thing is needed.*"

And then as you live life **one day** at a time, taking it **one step** at a time and doing only **one thing** at a time, you ask God to help you. Don't you try to deal with your stress alone. You allow the Lord to help you.

Now I want you to notice something that is very interesting about our text. There is a chapter division that separates chapter 10 from 11, but in the original manuscript there was not a chapter division. Immediately following this experience of Jesus with Martha, the disciples recognized a need in their lives, and they asked Jesus to help them. Look at Luke 11:1 as the disciples said to Jesus "Lord, teach us to pray." In other words, in dealing with their stress they needed help, and they knew Jesus could help them, and so they said to Him, "Lord, teach us to pray. Lord, help us."

Right now, if you are dealing with stress in your life you ask God to help you. I believe Mary found this peace in the *place* of her home because Jesus was there. He was with her in that sacred and reverential and holy *place*. Right now, in this "*place of quiet rest near to the heart of God*," you ask Him to help you live **one day** at a time, take **one step** at a time, do **one thing** at a time, and ask Him to help you overcome the stress and anxiety and worry in your life.

Allow God to minister to you through the beautiful words of this hymn:

> *There is a place of quiet rest,*
> *Near to the heart of God;*
> *A place where sin cannot molest,*
> *Near to the heart of God.*
>
> *There is a place of comfort sweet,*
> *Near to the heart of God;*
> *A place where we our Savior meet,*
> *Near to the heart of God.*
>
> *There is a place of full release,*
> *Near to the heart of God,*
> *A place where all is joy and peace,*
> *Near to the heart of God.*
>
> *O Jesus, blest Redeemer*
> *Sent from the heart of God,*
> *Hold us who wait before thee*
> *Near to the heart of God.*

Chapter 5

Joseph: Shriveling Away in the Land of Fear

"..Joseph was a righteous, just, and good (δίκαιος) man..."
Matthew 1:19
"...he was afraid (ἐφοβήθη)..."
Matthew 2:22a
Matthew 2:13-15, 19-22
Good People in Bad Places

We are doing a series of sermons on *Good People in Bad Places.* We are observing the lives of some **good people** who found themselves in **bad places**, and the interesting thing is that we find these **bad places** all around us in this modern day.

The title of our message for this sermon is **Joseph: Shriveling Away in the Land of Fear**. We are building this sermon upon two verses, and it is the margin between these two verses that I want us to occupy with our thinking.

First, in Matthew 1:19, the text tells us that "Joseph was a just man, a righteous man and *a good man.*" The Greek word that we translate "just" is the word *(δίκαιος)*, and this word refers to the goodness and righteousness of Joseph.

But secondly, Joseph found himself in a *bad place* as our second text, Matthew 2:22 simply says of Joseph, "and he was afraid."

Allow me to set the background for our text.

After the birth of Jesus, Herod sent out a decree to kill all children two years of age and younger. Joseph and Mary fled to Egypt, and in Matthew 2, verse 19 tells us that upon the death of Herod, an angel appeared to Joseph in a dream telling him to return to Israel.

Verse 21 tells us they came back to Israel.

Verse 22 tells us that Joseph heard that Archelaus, the son of Herod, was reigning, and in the next verse we find our text as it tells us that Joseph was *afraid* to go to Bethlehem in Judea, so he went to Galilee and Nazareth, and the verse that I want you to

50

note is verse 22 as it tells us that Joseph was afraid. For him, Bethlehem was *a place of fear*.

It is interesting to study the Christmas story and observe how many people were gripped with fear. Herod was fearful, and that's the reason he ordered that awful decree. Luke 1:6 tells us that Elizabeth and her family members were afraid. Luke 2:9 tells us that the Shepherds were afraid.

And Joseph was afraid. Yes, for him Judea was a place of fear, and he was indeed *a good man in a bad place*.

We don't hear a lot of sermons about Joseph. During the Christmas season we hear many stories about Mary, the mother of Jesus. Our friends in the Greek Orthodox tradition refer to her as the *Mega Theotokos*, the "Great Mother of God," and in these traditions, Mary occupies much of the attention, and she is especially venerated by these friends.

During the Advent and Christmas season we hear many sermons about the Baby Jesus. We hear many sermons about the wise men and the angels and shepherds. We hear many sermons about the inn keeper and how he had no room for the Baby Jesus.

I recently read about a concerned mother who called the church office on the afternoon before the Annual Christmas Play. She called to inform the office that her little boy who was to play the part of Joseph in the presentation was sick in bed with the flu, and he would not be able to be there. The director decided it was too late to get a substitute, so she simply wrote Joseph out of the script, and no one even noticed that Joseph was not there.

Someone has written these words about Joseph:
Of all the Creche characters, Joseph is the most neglected. We expect the angels, the shepherds and sheep, the wise men and camels, the mother and Child, and the scene would not be complete without them. But Joseph could easily be erased from the picture.

What do we expect? Joseph was a carpenter, not a writer or singer. Nowhere in the Bible is a single word of his quoted. We could probably describe him as "ordinary", and no one gets very excited over such persons—except God! And when God spoke, Joseph understood and obeyed.

Joseph accepted one of the most unusual and questionable roles ever given to a man. He became a husband, attended the birth of the Child, arranged for their safety as they took refuge in Egypt, and later provided both a home and companionship for the Boy in Bethlehem. And he apparently died while his son was a young man.

The best description of Joseph is that of Matthew where he was called "a just man." That means Joseph was a good man and he lived to the best of his ability in a right relationship with God. He may be easily forgotten. He may be written out of the script or eased from the picture and not be missed. But when God invaded this earth, and Christmas came to Bethlehem, Joseph of Nazareth found his purpose within the greater purposes of God.

And so, I want us to think about Joseph for a few moments in this message. I want us to focus the spotlight of our attention upon this **good man** who was in the **bad place of fear**.

There are two observations I want to make about fear, and I want to make them against the background of Joseph and in the context of Christmas. I want us to see:

I.   **The Problem of Fear**
II.   **The Prescription for Fear**

I.   **The Problem of Fear**

Fear is a problem that negatively affects us. Fear renders

us ineffective and makes us nonproductive. In Matthew 25, Jesus tells The Parable of the Talents. He tells about a master who had three servants. He gave to one servant five talents, to another servant two talents, and to another servant one talent. The man with the five talents went out, and he multiplied his. The man with two talents went out, and he did the same. But the man with the one talent buried his. When the time of reckoning came, the master asked the servant why he buried his one talent, and the servant feebly responded by saying in verse 25, "I was afraid." Fear takes away our drive and initiative and it makes us nonproductive.

It was a hot July day and a farmer was dressed in his overalls. He was wearing a straw hat, smoking his corn cob pipe, and sitting on the front porch. A stranger came by and asked "How is your crop coming?" The farmer replied, "Ain't got none. Didn't plant none. Fraid of the drought." The stranger then asked, "How about potatoes?" The old farmer replied, "Ain't got none. Scared of tater bugs."

Finally the stranger asked "What did you plant?"

The old man replied, "Nothing, I just played it safe!"

And when we are fearful, it makes us want to play it safe and we end up accomplishing very little.

When an athlete is afraid, he will lose a game. When a team is fearful, they will lose.

In November of 2010, Auburn won one of the most exciting games over the University of Alabama in the Iron Bowl. In that game, Auburn was behind 0-24. Auburn caught fire in the second half, played great and ended up winning the game 28-27.

To be sure, Auburn played some great football that second half, but I found it interesting to hear a sports analyst on television say this about the second half. He said, "Yes, Auburn played great football, but it seemed that in that second half Alabama quit playing to win, and they were simply playing to keep from getting beat. They seemed fearful, and fear will beat you every time."

Now, I know a lot more about tennis than I do about

football, and I know there are two ways to play tennis. One, you can play aggressively, and rush the net and play to win. Or two, you can allow fear to set in and you can become tentative as you stay on the baseline and push and simply play to keep from getting beat, and in nearly every instance, when a player takes that second way, they always end up losing.

Yes, it is difficult for an athlete or an athletic team to win when they are fearful.

When a salesman is fearful, he is not going to make that sale, but when he is optimistic and enthusiastic and confident, people will want to buy the product he is selling.

If a student goes into an examination with fear, that student will not do well on the test. But if the student prepares and studies hard, and goes into the examination with confidence and courage, that student will do well.

Yes, fear is a huge problem in our world today.

I read where a psychiatrist said that over 90 percent of the psychological problems that his patients dealt with were caused either directly or indirectly by fear. Yes, fear is a problem.

Henry David Thoreau, a transcendentalist writer said, "Nothing is so much to be feared as fear."

President Franklin D. Roosevelt said, "The only thing we have to fear is fear itself."

Lloyd Douglas said, "If a person harbors fear, it makes you a landlord to a ghost."

The German Philosopher Heidegger said, "Ours is an era of angst," which means "fear" in German.

Fear is a problem and it affects all of us. But the main thing I want us to notice in this message is not *the problem of fear*, *but the prescription* **for** overcoming and defeating **fear**.

II.   The Prescription for Fear

When we get sick, we go to the doctor, and he will write a

prescription for us. We take that prescription, get it filled and when we do what the prescription tells us to do, then we get well.

Well I want to share with you a prescription for fear, and if you will take it, it will help you address and deal with and overcome the fear in your life. The greatest Christmas present you can give yourself is to take this prescription, understand it, and use it.

There are three parts to this prescription:

One, *analyze*. By that I mean you need to analyze the fear in your life, and you need to understand that fear is like stress. Actually, it is fear that causes stress.

But fear is very much like stress in that there is good fear and there is bad fear. Now good fear is our fear of God. The Bible tells us that we are to fear God. That does not mean that we are to be frightened or scared of Him, but what it means is that with a mystical and reverential and holy awe, we are to come into His presence and worship Him. That is good fear.

Oswald Chambers in his book, *The Highest Good*, writes, "The remarkable thing about fearing God is that when you fear God you fear nothing else, whereas if you do not fear God you fear everything else." That is good fear.

But bad fear is the fear that is detrimental to you. It is what point one in this message is all about. Bad fear is very problematic to your life, and what you need to do is to carefully analyze the fear in your life. You see, you cannot solve a problem until you know what that problem is. You break that problem of fear down and ask yourself these questions: "Why am I afraid? Where did this fear come from? How is it affecting me? What is the reason for it? What can I do about it?" And so, the first part of the prescription is to **analyze** your fear.

Two, *realize* and by that I mean you realize what fear is capable of doing to you. You need to understand that bad fear can destroy you mentally, emotionally, spiritually and even physically.

I read a tragic story about a railway employee in Russia who accidentally locked himself in a refrigerator car. He could not escape, and although he beat upon the door he could not attract the attention of those on the outside. So this man resigned himself to his fate.

As the man felt his body becoming numb, he reported the story of his approaching death in sentences which he wrote on the wall of the car. He wrote, *"I am becoming colder…still colder, now nothing to do but wait…I am slowly freezing to death… half asleep now and I can hardly write…"* And then finally, *"these may be my last words."*

A short while later the door to the car was opened and the man was found dead and those were indeed his last words. What is interesting is that the freezing apparatus was out of order and the temperature of the car was only 56 degrees. There was no physical reason for his death. There was plenty of air, but he had suffocated. He was a victim of his own fear. Don't you see, fear cannot only break your heart and wreck your mind, but it can destroy your physically.

Three, *maximize*. By that I mean you must maximize your faith if you are to overcome the fear in your life. I believe you maximize your faith by expanding your faith, and you do it by living in the light of *II Timothy 1:7*. This verse says, "God has not given us the spirit of fear, but of power and love and a sound mind."

Notice this verse plainly tells us that fear is not of God. God did not give you that spirit of fear that you are nursing in your life right now, but God does give to you a triad of graces that are lifted up in this verse. There are three things you need from this verse to maximize your faith.

First, **power**. This verse tells us that God gives to us power. Through His Spirit, you let His grace give you joy and enthusiasm and excitement and purpose and meaning, and it will enable you in a powerful way to live above the problems and fears of life.

Secondly, **love**. God has given to us the spirit of love. It is the Greek word *agape*. In the midst of your fear, right now, you resolve to love yourself more. When you love yourself more you begin to build up your self-confidence, and that helps you overcome fear. You love yourself more. You love God more. You resolve to give Him all your love and affection and you love Him with all your heart, soul, and mind. You love other people. Much of your fear will be caused by other people and the more you fear that person who makes you fearful, then the worse your life is going to be. Instead of fearing that person, you try loving that person and see what happens.

Thirdly, a **sound** mind. The Greek word that we translate as a sound mind is from the Greek root *sophron*, and it is a term that literally means to discipline yourself. Some of the translations render that particular part of this verse as **self-discipline**. This is very important because ultimately that is where fear is controlled. It is controlled in your mind, so you must allow God's Spirit to control your mind if you are to overcome the fear in your life. You ask Him to give to you the mind of Christ, and you discipline yourself to live in that mindset, and you will overcome the fear in your life.

Our Lord wants to control our minds. That is the reason He came into this world. He wants to take away our fear and give to us peace and joy. This is the way our Lord came, and this is why He came. This hymn of Christmas reminds us of this truth. Listen attentively to these words as we sing them from the depths of our hearts:

Joy to the world, the Lord is come!
Let earth receive her King;
Let every heart prepare him room,
And heaven and nature sing,
And heaven and nature sing,
And heaven and heaven, and nature sing.

He rules the world with truth and grace,
And makes the nations prove,
The glories of his righteousness,
And wonders of his love,
And wonders of his love,
And wonders, wonders of his love.

Chapter 6

John the Baptist: Stumbling Around in the Prison of Doubt

"When John heard in prison what Christ was doing, he sent his disciples to ask Him, 'Are You the one to come, or should we expect someone else?'"
Matthew 11:2-3
Matthew 11:1-3
Good People in Bad Places

In this message I want to do the next sermon in our series: *Good People in Bad Places*. Sometimes **good people** have a way of getting into **bad places**. In this series of sermons we are looking at the lives of men and women in the Bible who found themselves in these places. We are looking at *good people* who found themselves in these *bad places*. We are studying the scriptural background of each one of these people, and then we are seeking to make a relevant application of their lives to our lives today.

Thus far we have talked about these **good people** in these **bad places**: **Elijah**: Sitting Under the Juniper Tree of **Discouragement**; **David**: Strolling Upon the Rooftop of Self-Ease; **Euodia and Syntyche**: Squabbling in the **Ring of Wrangling**; **James and John**: Strutting on the Slippery Slope of **Pride**; **Simon Peter**: Sinking in the Stormy Sea of **Fear**; **Martha**: Stressing Out in the Kitchen of **Worry**; **Joseph**: Shriveling Away in the Land of **Fear**; **The Paralytic Man**: Sorrowing on the Rooftop of **Disability**; **Gideon**: Sharing an Honest Question Under the Oak Tree of **Bewilderment**; **A Nameless Young Man**: Succumbing to an **Addiction** on the Far Side of Jordan; **Asa**: Standing Up to the **Enemy** in the Valley of Zephathah; **Jairus**: Struggling with **Grief** in His Own Home; **The Ten Disciples**: Succumbing to **Anger** in the Presence of Jesus; **Simon of Cyrene**: Straining Beneath **The Cross** on the Via Dolorosa; **Thaddaeus**: Side Stepping an **Awful Name** (one of his other names was Judas); **Jacob**: Skirmishing with God Down by the **Riverside**; **Paul and Silas**: Singing in the Prison of

Pain and Persecution Up in Philippi; **Paul**: Sizing Up the State of **Rejection** in a Roman Prison Cell; and **Peter**: Shrugging Off the **Negatives** in Rome.

My wife asked me, "How many more sermons are you going to preach in this series?" I told her I was going to keep preaching them until I ran out of people in the Bible who had problems or verbs that begin with the letter **S**.

I am doing this series of sermons for five reasons. One, to show us that these problems are not new. Two, to show us that **good people** find themselves in these **bad places** and face these **bad problems**. Three, to show us there are biblical models for addressing these issues. Four, to show us there are theological solutions to these problems. Five, to show us that our faith can help us answer these difficult questions of life.

Let me set the background for our message today. John the Baptist was a fiery prophet of old, and he was a mighty man of God. He proclaimed a flaming Gospel, and people responded to his message. And then all of a sudden—he was arrested. While he was languishing in that prison cell, we find the words of our text in Matthew 11:2-3 as it tells us, *"When John heard in prison what Christ was doing, he sent his disciples to ask Him: 'Are You really the one who was to come, or should we expect someone else?'"*

Tell me, have you ever found yourself in the prison of doubt? Come on and nod your heads. I don't want to have to preach on lying next Sunday. The truth of the matter is we all have doubts, and these doubts are a part of life, and they are a part of our faith. But when we let those doubts take away our confidence, it is then that those doubts begin to master us.

In this simple message, I want to share with you three areas where we all tend to doubt, and then in conclusion I want to show you what we can do with these doubts and how we can effectively master them.

We doubt:

I. **Our Selves**
II. **Other People**
III. **Our Faith**

I. Our Selves

I can understand why John the Baptist's self-esteem and confidence were so low. Prison is an awful place. Not only are there physical prisons for the body, but there are mental prisons of the mind—and one mental prison is self-doubt.

My friend, don't you doubt yourself. You are important, and you are special. The Psalmist tells us that, *"we are wonderfully made,"* and we are very precious to God.

I read about a third grade teacher who was instructing his class on new and recent scientific and technological developments. He said to the class, "Boys and girls, tell me something important that is in the world today that was not here ten years ago." One little boy in the back raised his hand, jumped up and shouted, "Me, Teacher, ME!" And that little boy was right on target because he is important, and he has made this a better world in which to live.

It is amazing what we can accomplish when we truly believe in ourselves, and it is also amazing what we fail to accomplish when we doubt ourselves.

During the Civil War, Rear Admiral DuPont failed to take his ships into Charleston Harbor. Admiral Farragut asked him why he did not take his ships into the harbor. DuPont responded with a good reason, and then Farragut said to him, "Admiral, that is a good explanation. But you and I both know the real reason you did not take your ships into the harbor was because you did not believe you could do it." Yes, it is amazing what you cannot do when you do not believe in yourself.

Oh friend, don't doubt yourself, but believe in yourself.

I saw a cute bumper sticker the other day. The grammar is

not all that good, but the theology is not all that bad. It simply said, "You are special. You are important. Because God don't make no junk."

Don't doubt yourself, but believe in yourself and what you can accomplish.

II.   Other People

In prison you are not around up-standing people and model citizens, and there are some people of whom you need to be cautious

I remember when we were living in Saraland, a community north of Mobile, Alabama. One of my closest friends was the Chief of Police, Chief Frank Pridgen. Chief Pridgen was not a member of my Church, but we became very dear friends. I remember that I would ride with him in his patrol car and we spent many hours talking as we rode around that part of Mobile County. Many times we rode together on Saturday night. He appointed me as the Chaplain to the Police Department, and it was such an honor and joy to be in ministry to so many of those fine police officers. I conducted many of their weddings and funerals.

A minister friend asked Chief Pridgen if he knew me. Chief Pridgen said, "Yes, I do. Brother Mathison is in our jailhouse nearly every Saturday night." It was such a joy to serve as the Chaplain to the Police Department. From the perspective of that chaplaincy, I saw a side of that community I never knew existed. It was totally different from my church experiences.

I remember Chief Pridgen called me one day and asked if I would visit a lady who was in jail. He told me that she had repeatedly asked to see a minister. I went to see her.

I'll never forget the way she looked. Her hair was in a bun; she did not have on any make-up; and I thought she was one of the sweetest looking ladies I had ever seen. In her lap was a shawl, and resting upon that shawl was an open Bible. She looked at me and said, "Reverend, I am so depressed in this jail. I want to get out and go and visit my mother." As she talked, she began to weep. I was so touched and moved that tears came to my eyes. I began to weep also.

I remember when I looked at her, she reminded me of a minister's wife—**not** because she was plain, simple and homely looking, but **because** she was sweet and kind and had an open Bible in her lap.

I left the jail cell and told Chief Pridgen that I did not feel she should be in jail. I said, "Chief, I'm not telling you how to run your business, but that lady does not need to be in jail. She is one of the sweetest ladies I've ever met, and her story moved me to tears. If you will let her out, my wife and I will do what we can to help her get on her feet and get started. We will even take her into our home."

I remember Chief Pridgen looked at me and said, "George, I'm not telling you how to run your business either, but let me tell you about her. Her boyfriend is also in jail. She is from one of the western states. This past Tuesday evening she and her boyfriend were driving down Interstate 65. They pulled off the interstate, and they stopped in front of a convenience store. Her boyfriend went in to rob the store. She sat in the car with the motor running and the windows down. When her boyfriend went in, because he was suspicious looking, the store clerk immediately pushed an emergency button that alerted the police. A patrol car was in the vicinity, and the car pulled up behind her vehicle. Two officers got out and approached her car with one on each side. The officer on her side of the car noticed that she had a shawl in her lap. He noticed something under the shawl, and he immediately grabbed it. When he did, it was a pistol that went off. It was a high-powered gun that blew a huge hole in the top of the car."

And then Chief Pridgen looked at me and said, "George, that is one of the most violent women we've ever had in our jail. There are two western states that have warrants for her and her boyfriend's arrest for assault and armed robbery. She is a dangerous woman!"

Well, I found out, there are those who will deceive you.

There are people who will hurt you and disappoint you and let you down; but if you are not careful, you will begin to doubt the motivation and intention of *every* person you meet.

As a part of my simple theology I believe that a part of God's grace is within every person. John Wesley called it prevenient grace, and it is the grace that goes before to prepare the way for saving and redeeming and sanctifying grace.

I also believe, as our friends in the Quaker tradition believe, that there is a spark of God that burns within every person. I also strongly believe that people have an amazing capacity for generosity, kindness and goodness if they are given a chance, and usually people respond to us on the level of our trust and confidence in them.

But still, it is so easy to doubt other people.

III.   Our Faith

I've carefully studied this text, and I believe that as John was stumbling around in that prison cell he doubted **himself**. I believe he was wondering to himself, "If I am such a great preacher and outstanding leader—then what am I doing in this prison?"

I also believe John was beginning to doubt **other people**, and my friend, when you doubt yourself and you begin to doubt others, then it is very easy for you to doubt **your faith in God**.

At this point, we need to learn an important lesson about doubt, and that is—when we doubt, we need to *do* something about it. I want you to notice that John the Baptist *did* something about it. He sent his disciples to ask Jesus, "Are You really the Messiah, or should we look for another?"

In the midst of our doubt, like John the Baptist, *we* need to *do* something about those doubts. When we doubt ourselves and other people and our faith, we need to *do* something positive about that doubt.

In closing, I want to suggest four things we need to **do** if we find ourselves stumbling around in the prison of doubt. We need to:

One, focus on **our** strengths.

Within all of us there are gifts, graces and talents, and within all of us there are also faults, failures and limitations. We can either focus on the positives, or we can focus upon the negatives. If we focus upon the failures of the past, and the negative flaws that are evident in our lives today, then we will lose confidence and doubt ourselves and cast a dark cloud over tomorrow. But if we focus upon God's goodness and grace in our lives and our strengths, then we will gain confidence and we will believe in ourselves.

Two, we need to look for the best in **other** people.

When you look at other people, don't judge them, but celebrate the positives in their lives. In every person we can find the bad if we are looking for it, but on the other hand we can also find good in every person if we are looking for it. Dr. Pierce Harris said:

> *There is so much good in the worst of us,*
> *And so much bad in the best of us;*
> *It hardly behooves any of us*
> *To go and judge the rest of us.*

Instead of judging people, you celebrate the good in them, and you will begin to believe in them.

Three, **ask** questions.

That is exactly what John the Baptist did. He sent his disciples to ask Jesus if He was truly the Messiah.

You remember when Thomas was in the Upper Room, he was filled with doubt. And in a questioning way he looked at Jesus and said, "Except I put my fingers into the scar and nail prints, I will not believe." Then Jesus looked at Thomas and invited him to do precisely that. Thomas did, and his doubts were allayed as he responded with that powerful affirmation, *"My Lord and My God."*

You see, sincere questions lead to religious certainty.

Honest query leads to theological truth.

64

Don't you ever be afraid to ask questions because those questions are the pathway that lead to ultimate confidence and a stable faith.

Four, learn to **doubt your doubts**.

We do a pretty good job of doubting ourselves, and doubting other people, and especially doubting our faith, and doubting God, but have you ever thought about doubting your doubts? Very few people have.

One of the most prolific writers of the 1940s and 1950s was Dr. A. J. Cronin. He wrote many inspirational books such as: *The Keys of the Kingdom* and *The Citadel*. He was sort of the Max Lucado and Rick Warren of his day. Many of Cronin's books were even represented in film.

Something interesting about Cronin was the fact that writing was only a hobby for him. By profession, he was a physician.

Something even more interesting about Cronin is that during his days in medical school he wanted very much to become a surgeon. That was the great dream of his heart. One of his major professors and mentors told him that he should not plan to be a surgeon because he had practically no dexterity in his hands. He immediately doubted his ability to be a surgeon, and he followed the advice of the professor.

Upon graduating from medical school he went to a small village in the Scottish Highlands, and there he opened his practice. One night during a blizzard a tree fell across a young man and seriously injured his spine. Without a delicate, neurological operation, he would be paralyzed. His parents begged Cronin to operate, but he remembered what his medical professor told him.

Then something happened. Cronin later wrote, "For the first time I questioned the validity of that man's verdict...doubts and fears were swept away. I *knew* I could operate successfully, and with God's help, I did."

And thus he transcended his doubts, fears, and feelings of inadequacy and inferiority, and he not only enabled a young boy to walk, but he gained a renewed faith and confidence for the first time.

This morning, do you find yourself, like John the Baptist, stumbling around in the prison of doubt? Do you doubt yourself, other people and your faith? If so, I'll challenge you to take these four steps, and beginning now—you focus upon your strengths, you look for the best in other people, you ask questions, and you begin to doubt those doubts that have hung like a dark cloud over you for so long, and like John the Baptist, you will find true confidence, and you will walk out of that dark prison into the bright sunlight of a liberating and genuine faith.

Section II

Biblical Principles by Which I Daily Live

Chapter 7

Trust God
"Trust in the Lord and do good; dwell in the land
and you shall enjoy safe pasture and be fed."
Psalm 37:3
First Sermon in Series: ***Biblical Principles by Which I Daily Live***

Today I want to do the first of four sermons on the theme *Biblical Principles by Which I Daily Live*. These principles are found in Psalm 37, and everyday I seek to live by these four principles. They govern my life, and they give spiritual, theological, motivational, personal and practical direction to my life daily.

Next Sunday we will look at the second message as it will be entitled **Happiness Is a Choice**, and it will be based upon Psalm 37:4 when the Psalmist says, *"Delight yourself in the Lord, and He will give to you the desires of your heart."*

The third message will be entitled **"Not Acceptable!"** and it will be taken from Psalm 37:27 when the Psalmist says, *"Depart from evil, do good and live forever more."*

And the fourth sermon will be entitled **Love and Kindness are the Most Important Things in the World**, and it will be based upon Psalm 37:37 when the Psalmist says, *"Mark the perfect man; behold the upright, for the end of that person is peace."* It is my interpretation of this verse that it is a prophetic reference to Jesus Christ because He was the only perfect person who ever lived, and He was the very embodiment of love and kindness.

As we study these four principles, I want you to notice the first principle is upward and vertical in its application as we look to God and trust Him. Principles two and three are inward in their application as they teach us how to get along with ourselves. The fourth principle is outward and horizontal and relational as it tells us how to relate and get along with other people and how we should treat them. Out of a heart of love, we must always extend kindness to everybody.

The message today is **Trust God**, and I want to share with you five areas of my life that I daily entrust to God. I trust God daily with my:

I. **Faith**
II. **Faults**
III. **Finances**
IV. **Family**
V. **Fears**

I.   **Faith**

I have a very simple faith. It seems that the more I've studied and grown theologically and spiritually, the simpler my faith has become.

I remember when I became a Christian and when I started to college, it seemed that my faith was somewhat complicated, rigid and set in stone. Christologically, soteriologically and eschatologically I had the most elaborate systematic scheme of theology. I knew what I believed, and I knew that I was right, and people who did not completely agree with me—they were wrong. But the more I've studied and matured in my faith, it seems the simpler my faith has become. When I finished my post doctoral studies at Yale, I realized that my faith is very simple.

I understand now what Soren Kierkegaard meant when he said, "Oh blessed simplicity, that seizes swiftly what cleverness, tired out in the service of vanity, may grasp slowly."

And that blessed simplicity characterizes my faith.

There are some simple things that I believe, but I believe them with all of my heart.

One, I believe that God loves me. I have difficulty fathoming how He can love me, but I believe He does love me.

I understand what George Beverly Shea meant when he penned these words:

There's the wonder at sunrise at morning;
The wondrous sunset I see;
But the wonder of wonders that thrills my soul
Is the wonder that God loves me.
Oh, the wonder of it all, the wonder of it all;
The wonder that God loves me.

Yes, I believe that God loves me and that I am very precious to His heart.

Two, I believe God sent His Son Jesus Christ into this world to save and sanctify me. I believe that in Christ I find my salvation and my sanctification.

Three, I believe that God, through Jesus Christ, is with me every step of the way. I don't believe He ever leaves me, and He is always by my side. I believe Him when He says, *"I will never leave you nor forsake you, and I will be with you until the end of the age."* I believe He is with me in everything I do.

Four, I believe that when I die, God has a place in heaven for me. That is what Jesus meant in John 14 when He said, "In my Father's house are many mansions." The Greek word we translate "mansion" is the word "mona" (*μοναὶ*) and it literally means "a room." Yes, "In my Father's house are many rooms, and I go to prepare your place." The Greek word we translate as "place" is the word topou (*τόπου*), and it means an "actual and real place." When I come to the end of life's journey on this earth, I believe that God will send His Angel to take my soul into the very presence of God and to be with Him eternally in heaven.

I am reading the most fascinating book. It is the biography of Dietrich Bonhoeffer, and it is entitled **Bonhoeffer: Pastor, Martyr, Prophet, Spy.** It chronicles the life of Bonhoeffer. The author is Eric Metaxas who is Greek Orthodox. I am in the early part of the book where it chronicles the education of Bonhoeffer. It tells of his studies at The University of Tubingen and The University of Berlin. Bonhoeffer tells of the tremendous influence Karl Barth had upon his life and how Barth impacted his theology. Bonhoeffer refers to Barth as "the greatest theologian," and in my theological studies I was so impressed and enamored by Barth.

Karl Barth was once lecturing in the United States, and he was at Princeton University. Following an intellectually deep academic presentation, he held a "Question and Answer" period. One student asked Barth this question: "What is the profoundest theological truth you've ever learned?" Those who were present said that tears came to the eyes of Karl Barth as he said, "The greatest theological truth I've ever learned was taught to me sitting upon my mother's knee when she sang to me, 'Jesus loves me, this I know; for the Bible tells me so.'"

Yes, I have a very simple faith. Notice I did not say "simplistic." There is a difference between simplistic and simple. While my faith is simple, I hope that it has depth; and I trust God daily with my simple faith.

II.   Faults

I try so hard to, as our text says, to "do good," but there are times that I just royally mess up. There are times that I stumble and fall, but it is precisely during those times that I trust my Savior to reach out with His loving arms and lift me, pick me up, and help me go a little higher the next time.

You see, we are going to fall. We are going to make mistakes, and we are going to sin.

I John 1 speaks of our faults and how God helps us overcome those faults when we trust Him. Notice verse 8 of I John 1 says, *"If we say we have no sin, then we deceive ourselves and the truth is not in us."* We are going to sin, and we are going to make mistakes and we are going to fall, but notice, when we trust God, verse 9 tells us what He will do. It says, *"If we confess our sins, He is faithful and just to forgive us and to cleanse us from all unrighteousness."*

Yes, when I stumble, fall and fail, it is during those times that I trust His forgiving and loving and redemptive presence, and

71

I know He always forgives and helps me do better.

III. Finances

I trust Him with my finances. In these economic hard times, I know He is in control and He will meet my every need.

My wife and I were raised in strong Methodist families where we were taught the importance of tithing. For us, like prayer, Bible study and worship, tithing is a means of growing in grace and through this spiritual discipline, we feel His presence in our lives. Tithing has always been a very important part of our faith, and I believe that when we honor God with our finances, then He will meet our every need.

I understand what the Psalmist meant when he said, *"I have never seen the righteous forsaken, nor his children begging bread."*

In Proverbs 3, the two threads that run through the fabric of that chapter are: one, trusting God, and two, handling our finances, and that is precisely what we are looking at under point three.

Notice, Proverbs 3:5 speaks of trusting God as it says, *"Trust in the Lord with all your heart and do not lean to your own understanding."* And then verse 6 says, *"In all your ways acknowledge Him, and He will direct your path."*

When we trust God with our finances, notice what the writer of Proverbs says in verse 9. He says, *"Honor the Lord with your substances and the **first fruits** of all your increase,"* and when we do, verse 10 says, *"...and your barns and your wine presses will be filled with plenty."* I believe with all of my heart that when I trust God and allow Him to direct my path, then in His faithfulness He will care for me and meet my need.

And you know, if I can't trust God with my finances and money that will diminish and decay and fade into oblivion, then how can I trust Him with my immortal soul that will live forever?

Yes, I trust Him with my finances.

IV. Family

When I get to heaven, there are three questions I want to ask God.

First, "Why did You call me into the ministry?" Now, with that question I am not trying to display some mock-humility, but I cannot fathom why God would call me to preach His unsearchable riches to a hurting world. I believe the ministry is the highest, noblest, and most sacred calling. Dr. Dennis Kinlaw who was the President of Asbury College said, "If God has called you to preach, then don't stoop to become a king."

I am so humbled that He called me into the ministry, and although I can't completely understand it, I am looking forward to Him explaining it to me someday.

Secondly, I would ask, "Why did You allow me to marry such a wonderful person like Monteigne?" She is the most perfect person I have ever met, and I shutter to think where I would be if she had not come into my life.

When I finish this series of sermons on *Biblical Principles by Which I Daily Live*, I want to do a series of sermons on *Secrets to the Happiest Marriage on Earth*, because I honestly feel that God has blessed us with the happiest and most blessed marriage on earth.

We are living in a day when one out of every two marriages ends in divorce. When I preach these sermons, I especially want our university students to know that marriage **can** indeed be "a haven of blessing and a place of bliss."

But I wonder, why did God allow me the privilege and joy of sharing my life with this wonderful person?

Thirdly, "Why did You allow us to have such a wonderful daughter like Mallory?"

I remember right after our daughter was born, I was very worried about her. I know that in this imperfect world there are so many trials and temptations that face a pretty little girl. I never will forget when she was just a little baby, one night I was worrying about her and her future. I could not sleep. I got up, went into her room and knelt by her little crib and took her hand. I remember it as though it were yesterday. I simply committed her into the arms of Jesus and I said, "Lord, I trust You with her, and I am giving her to You." I remember a sweet peace just flooded my heart and covered me.

Now, I'm not saying that she hasn't given me a gray hair or two over the years, but I am so thankful for her.

Yes, each day I trust God with my family.

V.   Fears

I trust God with my fears.

Fear expresses itself in four ways. It expresses itself through anxiety, worry, stress and a lack of confidence.

I wish I could stand before you right now and tell you that I am never fearful and I don't ever worry, but I've found that when I commit those fears and worries to God, and I completely trust Him with them, then life is so much easier and I am so much happier.

The Bible says, *"Not a sparrow falls to the ground without His noticing it,"* and if His eye is on that little sparrow, then I know He is watching me, and I daily trust Him.

Elizabeth Cheney wrote:
> *Said the robin to the sparrow,*
> *"Why do these human beings*
> *Hurry round and worry so?"*
> *"I don't know,"*
> *Said the sparrow to the robin,*
> *"I don't know;"*
> *"But I think it must be,*
> *That these human beings*
> *Have no Heavenly Father*
> *Such as cares for you and me."*

Oh we do have a Heavenly Father who cares for us, and He wants us to trust Him with our fears and our worries.

My brother John Ed preached for us on Christmas Eve, and in his sermon he made reference to a book he recently wrote entitled *Transformed Living in Tough Times.*

In this book John Ed tells of growing up as a PK. A "PK" is a "preacher's kid." We have many PKs in our church. Like my brother, I am one.

In the churches my father served early in his ministry, the parsonage was always next door to the church.

One of the first churches he served was in Rosinton down in Baldwin County, Alabama. It is interesting that when my dad was the pastor there he received into the membership and baptized Dewey Northcutt who is a member of our church now. That was the beginning of a wonderful friendship between my dad and Brother Dewey, and Brother Dewey has become one of my closest friends.

When Dad was the pastor at Rosinton, one day my mother and he could not find John Ed. John Ed must have been about three or four years old. They heard a noise over in the church next door to the parsonage, and they went into the sanctuary and they saw John Ed. He had pulled a chair up behind the pulpit, placed several song books on the chair, and he was standing there behind the pulpit flaying his little arms in the air shouting at the top of his voice, "Be good, folks! Be good, folks!" And then with perfect precision, he raised his little chubby arms and in his best ministerial tone said, "And now we will receive the morning offering!"

When we lived in Wetumpka, the parsonage was also next to the church. In this book, John Ed tells of how when he was six years of age dad would ask him on Saturday nights sometimes to go over to his office at the church. Dad would be in the parsonage studying his sermon for the next day, and he would ask John Ed to get a book or a certain paper. John Ed said that was always such a frightening experience. He said that when he got to the church he could barely reach the light switch and he was scared to death. He heard all kinds of strange noises.

John Ed said that one Saturday night our dad asked him to go over to his office at the church. John Ed looked at our father and said, "Daddy, I don't want to walk over there alone. Would you please take my hand and walk with me?"

His loving father reached out, took the hand of his child, and together they started to walk into the dark night. John Ed said that as they walked, all fear was gone and there was a deep courage and calm peace in his heart as he walked along beside a father whom he loved and **trusted**.

As we walk into this week, there are two questions I want to ask you.

One, this week will you trust God? Will you trust Him with your faith, your faults, your finances, your family, and your fears?

And two, beginning right now, will you put your hand in His mighty hand and as you walk into the uncertainty of this week, will you walk next to Him holding His strong hand?

Our closing hymn was written by Thomas Dorsey, and it challenges us to walk through life holding His hand. We will remain seated as we softly sing the first two verses, and then stand as we sing the third. Allow these words to minister to you:

>*Precious Lord, take my hand,*
>*Lead me on, let me stand,*
>*I am tired, I am weak, I am worn;*
>*Through the storm, through the night,*
>*Lead me on to the light:*
>*Take my hand, precious Lord,*
>*Lead me home.*
>
>*When my way grows drear,*
>*Precious Lord, linger near,*
>*When my life is almost gone,*
>*Hear my cry, hear my call,*
>*Hold my hand lest I fall:*
>*Take my hand, precious Lord,*
>*Lead me home.*

When the darkness appears
And the night draws near,
And the day is past and gone,
At the river I stand,
Guide my feet, hold my hand:
Take my hand, precious Lord,
Lead me home.

Chapter 8

Happiness Is a Choice

*"Delight (**anag**) yourself in the Lord, and He will*
give you the desires of your heart."
Psalm 37:4
Psalm 37:3-4
Second Sermon in Series: ***Biblical Principles by Which I Daily Live***

This is the second of four sermons in our series of messages on the theme: ***Biblical Principles by Which I Daily Live***. These principles are very personal with me, and they emanate from the very depths of my theology.

As I stated earlier, they govern my life. They give to me spiritual, theological, motivational, practical and personal direction each day.

Very briefly and compactly, let me share with you where we have been, where we are going, and where we are today.

We began this series of sermons with the first biblical principle which I entitled **Trust God**. It is taken from Psalm 37:3 when the Psalmist says, *"Trust in the Lord and do good; dwell in the land and you shall enjoy safe pasture and be fed."* In that sermon I said that I daily put my trust in God. I put my trust in Him afresh and anew every morning, and through the day I trust God with my faith, my faults, my finances, my family, and my fears.

Next Sunday morning we will do the third sermon in this series as I will entitle it **"Not Acceptable!"** And this message will be built upon Psalm 37:27 when the Psalmist says, *"Turn and depart from evil and do good; then you will live securely, yes, you will dwell in the land forever."*

As we live life, negative and destructive and deadly and harmful and painful thoughts will try to enter our minds and invade our psyches each day. These emotions can poison our souls, and they breed anxiety, worry, stress and depression. Next

Sunday morning I want to show you how you can eliminate these thoughts from your mind and live above them.

And then the fourth and final message will be **Love and Kindness are the Most Important Things in the World**, and this message will be based upon Psalm 37:37 when the Psalmist says, *"Mark the perfect man; behold the upright; for the end of that man is peace."*

I believe that is a prophetic reference to Jesus Christ because He was the only perfect person who ever lived; and He was the very embodiment of love—and out of that love proceeded kindness for everybody.

In this message, I want to show you how kindness on your part towards others can positively impact you. It can help you.

One, it can help you socially. I am going to show you how through this principle you can win friends and influence people.

Two, it can also help you in your business. In the business world it is so important to have education, expertise and experience—but I dare say that relationship skills are as important as all three of those put together, for if you can't get along with people and relate to people, then you are not going to succeed in the business world. This principle can help you immensely with your vocation.

And three, it can help you in your home. I am convinced that the greatest need within the home today is simply learning to be kind to one another, and I am going to show you how this principle can help you with your family and your home.

Now, I want you to notice the principle we've studied thus far. The first principle, *Trust God*, is vertical and upward as it shows us how to relate to and look to God.

The second and third principles are inward as they show us how to overcome and defeat the enemies of anxiety, stress, worry and negative thinking.

The fourth principle is outward or horizontal or relational because it tells us how to get along with one another, and all four of these principles are essential if we are going to be complete, fulfilled and victorious Christians.

Now for just a few moments let's look at the second principle, and like the third principle it is inward in its application because it speaks of happiness and self-contentment.

Our text is from Psalm 37:4 as the Psalmist says, *"Delight yourself in the Lord, and He will give you the desires of your heart."*

I want you to notice the word "delight." It is an action verb, and it implies that **you** must take the initiative and **you** must make it happen. Delight and happiness are your choice.

According to Professor Strong, this Hebrew word (*anag*) that we translate as delight means to be soft in spirit, to be pliable, to be joyful, and to be happy.

Against the background of our text, how can we be happy? If happiness is a choice, how do we choose this happiness?

I believe there are three steps in the process. To be happy we must:

I.   **Decide**
II.   **Determine**
III.   **Depend**

I.   **Decide**

First, we must decide to be happy. We must make it happen.

My friend, you decide whether you are going to be happy, and nobody else has that privilege. If you are unhappy today, it is because you chose to be unhappy. Oh, to be sure, external circumstances, emotions, events, people and the weather influence us, but the ultimate person who determines your happiness in your life is you and nobody else.

One of my heroes is Viktor Frankl. I'm sure you know he wrote the book, ***Man's Search for Meaning***.

Because he was a Jew, Frankl was placed in a concentration camp by the Nazis in WWII. In many ways, his is a very sad story. He lost his wife, his children, and his parents to the Holocaust.

When Frankl was put into the concentration camp, the first thing the Gestapo made him do was strip. Viktor Frankl stood there completely naked. They even cut away his wedding band.

It was then that Viktor Frankl with keen and great insight said to himself, "You can take away my parents; you can take away my wife; you can take away my children; you can take all of my material possessions; you can strip me of my clothes and you can even cut away my wedding band—but there is one thing no person can ever take away from me, and that is my freedom to choose how I will react to what happens to me."

Don't you see, happiness is a choice we make in life. Even though the outward circumstances may be harmful and painful, inwardly it can be peaceful and serene because we determine our happiness.

Yes, happiness is a choice.

If you choose, every day can be a happy day, and every day can be a good day.

I read about an elderly member in a church who taught his pastor a wonderful lesson when the minister casually wished him a "good day." This wise man immediately responded, "Reverend, they are all good days. It is what we put in them that changes them."

I remember one morning my wife and I were driving to the hospital to be with a family whose loved one was having surgery. I distinctly remember how it was raining and storming that day. As we were driving I casually remarked to my wife, "It is a *terrible* day. It is an *awful* day."

My sweet wife lovingly rebuked me. I don't know about you, but there are times that I need to be lovingly rebuked. There are probably times that I just need to be rebuked in any way. She is very positive, and she immediately responded, "No, it is not a bad day. It is not a terrible day. It is a good day. Yes, it is raining and cold outside, but it is a great day."

Tell me, are you choosing happiness today, and have you made this a good day? Are you making it a great day?

Yes, happiness is a choice and our decision determines what that choice will be.

II.   Determine

With your mind, you decide to be happy, and then with a dogged determination you make yourself happy.

You know, if we have a cold or the flu, we go to the doctor and he writes out a prescription for antibiotics that can permeate our system and make us well.

May I give you **a simple prescription for happiness**? Just as a doctor's prescription can help you physically, so this prescription for happiness can help you spiritually and emotionally. The simple prescription is this: *You decide and determine in your mind that you are going to be a happy person, and you choose this happiness. And so today, do it!*

In this world there are some people who have decided and they are determined to be unhappy. Now, I am sure there is nobody like that in this service, but there could be some watching by television. Now I do not want you to be left out, so let me share with you **a prescription for unhappiness** that I found in a newsletter that crossed my desk. Listen carefully:

1. *Make little things bother you; don't just let them, make them!*
2. *Lose your perspective on things, and keep it lost. Don't put first things first.*
3. *Get yourself a good worry—one which you cannot do anything about but worry over it. Then you just go get in a corner somewhere, sit down and you worry yourself sick.*
4. *Be a perfectionist; condemn yourself and others for not achieving perfection.*
5. *Be right. Be ALWAYS right. Perfectly right all the time. Be the only one who is right, and be rigid about your rightness.*
6. *Don't trust or believe people, or accept them at anything but their worst and weakest. Be suspicious. Impute ulterior motives to them.*
7. *Always compare yourself unfavorably to others, which is the guarantee of instant misery.*

8. *Take personally with a chip on your shoulder everything that happens to you and that you don't like. You must understand the world is against you, and it is going to get you one way or the other.*
9. *Do not give yourself whole-heartedly or enthusiastically to anything or anybody. You just stay wrapped up in yourself.*

If you use this prescription with regularity then you will be guaranteed unhappiness, but you just remember that it is your choice.

Or, you can choose, and with determination, you can be happy.

One of my dear friends in the ministry is Dr. Jesse Shackelford. In one of his newsletters he told about a dear 92 year old lady who is determined to be happy. Listen carefully as this will warm your heart:

> *The 92 year old, petite, well-poised and proud mother who is fully dressed each morning by eight o'clock with her hair fashionably coifed and makeup perfectly applied, even though she is legally blind, moved to a nursing home today. Her husband of 70 years recently passed away, making the move necessary. Maurine Jones is the most lovely, gracious, dignified woman you would ever want to meet.*
>
> *After many hours of waiting patiently in the lobby of the nursing home, she smiled sweetly when she was told her room was ready. As she maneuvered her walker to the elevator, the supervisor provided a visual description of her tiny room, including the eyelet sheets that had been hung on her window. "I love it," she stated with the enthusiasm of an 8 year old having just been presented with a new puppy.*
>
> *"Mrs. Jones, you haven't seen the room...just wait." "That doesn't have anything to do with it," she replied. "Happiness is something you decide*

on ahead of time, and then with determination you make that happiness a reality. Whether I like my room or not does not depend on how the furniture is arranged. It is how I arranged my mind. I have already decided to love it. I am determined to love it.

It is a decision I make every morning when I wake up. I have a choice. I can spend the day in bed recounting the difficulty I have with the parts of my body that no longer work, or get out of bed and be thankful for the ones that do. Each day is a gift, and as long as my eyes open, I'll focus on the new day and all the happy memories I've stored away—just for this time in my life."

Like that lady, are you determined to be happy? Friend, it is your choice.

III.   Depend

I want you to notice our text again. Notice there are two parts of it. The first part tells us that we ourselves must make ourselves happy because the text begins, "Delight yourself..." Now in Whom do we delight, and Who gives to us "...the desires of our heart?" Do circumstances give to us this happiness? Do events give to us this happiness? Do emotions give to us this happiness? Do people give to us this happiness? Does the weather give to us this happiness? Does our boss give to us this happiness? Do our wives or our husbands?

No! Notice it is the Lord who gives to us this happiness because the second part of our text says, "He (the Lord) will give to you the desires of your heart."

I remember when we were appointed to this great church in June of 1990. I was at Annual Conference at Huntingdon College, and immediately following the reading of the appointments, I was in the Julia Russell Dining Hall, and there I met the three Delegates from our church. They were three of the finest men

I've ever met, and they became three of my closest friends. They were Charles Rew, Ed Taylor, and Hoyt Roberts, and over the years I learned to love them as brothers.

All three of them now have outrun us to the Father's House. I had their funerals, and they are in heaven now.

When we were appointed to this church, Lester Spencer was our associate minister. Lester was not only our associate pastor, but he became one of the closest friends that I've ever had in this world. I remember how much fun it was just being in ministry with him everyday. It was very much then like it is with our present associate pastor, Brother Charles. Lester and I enjoyed so much doing things together. We spent much of our time visiting. Many times Lester would drive, and he would talk to me while he was driving. He would share with me wonderful ideas for sermons. I told him to keep his eye on the road. I remember one night while we were visiting and he was driving, I re-dedicated my life to the Lord three times that evening.

It was right after we moved here, I told Lester I wanted us to visit one of the delegates to the Conference whom I met. I told him I wanted us to visit Charles Rew.

I remember it as though it were yesterday. It was one evening about 9:00 p.m. that Lester and I went over and visited Charles and his wife and daughter in their home on Heard Street. I remember the Rews had a little feisty dog named Charlie. Charlie was the meanest little dog I've ever seen in my life. Now I love dogs, but for some reason Charlie and I did not connect. When he first looked upon me, he did not like me. When I first looked upon him, I did not like him. I remember we sat in the living room and we visited with the Rews, and that mean little dog never took his eyes off of me. He glared at me and would show his teeth.

My dear friend and christian brother Lester saw how the dog and I were looking at each other. The dog would growl and grit his teeth with a hateful stare directed only towards me.

And then brother Lester, my dear and faithful and loyal and trustworthy and honorable brother and associate pastor, looked into my eyes, and then he turned and looked into the eyes of Charlie the dog. He then looked at me again and glanced back

85

at Charlie again, and then with his eyes firmly fixed upon me he said in a loud voice, "Sic him, Charlie!"

I've never seen a little dog move so fast as he headed straight towards me. With eyes glaring, teeth glistening, and saliva flowing, I immediately leaped up in the chair. I jumped upon the back of the chair and I called upon the Name of my precious Lord for protection.

That was my first visit with Charles Rew. While I did not love his dog. I learned to love him like a brother and he became one of my dearest friends.

Last month on December 6, we had the funeral service for Brother Charles Rew. Really it was not a funeral service. It was a service of celebration, resurrection, remembrance and comfort. In his service I shared that illustration about Lester and the dog.

I also told the congregation that I thought Charles Rew was one of the happiest people I've ever met in my life. He always had a big smile. Charles had chosen to *decide* and *determine* to make himself happy; and he *depended* upon God to give to him "the desires of his heart" that led to happiness. In that service we celebrated the happiness that was such an inherent part of his life and that he shared with others.

An example of that happiness and the way Charles depended upon God was exemplified in a little essay that concluded the service. It was read by Rev. Donna Sue Waller. Donna Sue is a daughter of this church, and she is a minister in the South Georgia Conference.

The essay is entitled *Footprints—the New Version.* Now, like most ministers, I had shared that original story of *Footprints in the Sand* many times. It is a beautiful story to read, especially at funerals. But I had never heard the **new version.**

I want to close with this **new version** of *Footprints in the Sand* that Donna Sue read at Charles' service. Following the reading of this, we then will sing of happiness and joy and dancing with the nineteenth century Shaker tune and song, *Lord of the Dance.* Listen to these words:

Imagine you and the Lord Jesus are walking

down the road together. For much of the way the Lord's footprints go steadily, consistently, rarely varying the pace.

But your footprints are a disorganized stream of zig-zags, starts, stops, turn arounds, circles, departures and returns.

For much of the way, it seems to go like this, but gradually your footprints come more in line with the Lord's, soon paralleling His consistently.

You and Jesus are walking as true friends!

This seems perfect, but then an interesting thing happens: Your footprints that once etched the sand next to Jesus' are now walking precisely in His steps.

Inside His larger footprints are your smaller ones; you and Jesus are becoming one.

This goes on for many miles, but gradually you notice another change. The footprints inside the large footprints seem to grow larger.

Eventually they disappear altogether. There is only one set of footprints. They have become one.

This goes on for a long time, but suddenly the second set of footprints is back. This time it seems even worse! Zigzags all over the place. Stops. Starts. Gashes in the sand. A variable mess of prints.

You are amazed and shocked.

Your dream ends. Now you pray:

'Lord, I understand the first scene, with zigzags and fits. I was a new Christian; I was just learning. But You walked on through the storm and helped me learn to walk with You.'

"*That is correct.*"

'And when the smaller footprints were inside of Yours, I was actually learning to walk in Your steps, following You very closely.'

"*Very good. You have understood everything so far.*"

'When the smaller footprints grew and filled in

Yours, I suppose that I was becoming like You in every way.'

"Precisely."

'*So Lord, was there a regression or something? The footprints separated, and this time it was worse than at first.'*

There was a pause as the Lord answers, with a smile in His voice.

"You *didn't* **know???** *It was* **then** *that* **you** **chose to be happy.** *You depended upon Me, and* **together we danced!"**

Ecclesiastes 3:1 and 4 says, "To everything there is a season, a time for every purpose under heaven: A time to weep, a time to laugh and be happy; a time to mourn, and a time to *dance*."

Right now, will you choose to be happy?

Join with me as we sing together:

I danced in the morning when the world was begun,
And I danced in the moon and the stars and the sun,
And I came down from heaven and I danced on the earth.
At Bethlehem I had my birth.

I danced for the scribe and the Pharisee,
But they would not dance and they would not follow me;
I danced for the fishermen, for James and John;
They came to me and the dance went on.

I danced on the Sabbath when I cured the lame,
The holy people said it was a shame;
They whipped and they stripped and they hung me high;
And they left me there on a cross to die.

I danced on a Friday and the sky turned black;
It's hard to dance with the devil on your back;
They buried my body and they thought I'd gone,
But I am the dance and I still go on.

They cut me down and I leapt up high,
I am the life that'll never, never die;
I'll live in you if you'll live in me;
I am the Lord of the Dance, said he.

Chorus

Dance, then, wherever you may be;
I am the Lord of the Dance, said he.
And I'll lead you all wherever you may be,
And I'll lead you all in the dance, said he.

Chapter 9

"Not Acceptable!"

*"Turn and depart (**suwr**) from evil and do (**asah**) good; then you will live securely, yes you will dwell (**shakan**) in the land forever."*
Psalm 37:27
Third Sermon in Series: ***Biblical Principles by Which I Daily Live***

This is the third sermon in our series of messages in the series ***Biblical Principles by Which I Daily Live***. These four principles are very personal with me. They reflect my personal theology, and they govern my life daily.

Every morning when I awaken I read these four selections of Scripture, and I verbally state these four principles, and I seek to live by them as I go through the day.

As we seek to live life each day, negative thoughts, angry thoughts, bitter thoughts, deadly thoughts, destructive thoughts, harmful thoughts, and painful thoughts will daily try to enter our minds and invade our psyches; and these thoughts breed anxiety, stress and worry. They can poison our lives spiritually, emotionally, mentally, and even physically.

Just as we choose to be happy on the inside, so we must choose to keep these negative thoughts away from us on the outside. And the way we do that is to say, ***"Not Acceptable!"***

I must confess that the title for this sermon is not original with me.

Dr. Randy Pausch taught at the University of Virginia and then at Carnegie Mellon University. He contracted and died of pancreatic cancer. Randy inspired millions with his ***Last Lecture***, which was later put into book form. It is a lecture about achieving your childhood dreams.

Just prior to his death, Randy and his wife Jai were being interviewed by Diane Sawyer of ABC News. In that interview Jai told Ms. Sawyer that during stressful times when she would go into dark places, and negative thoughts would attempt to enter her mind, a part of her mantra was to say and repeat and believe the simple phrase, *"Not Necessary!"* Jai went on to say that the repeating of that statement helped her to live life fully.

I have taken that phrase of Jai and I have adapted it in two ways. First, to accommodate my personal theology and philosophical mantra, I have changed it to *"Not Acceptable!"* That is a little more emphatic, and that works best for me. Secondly, I've given to that statement a scriptural context and a spiritual application.

Now, to make this statement, *"Not Acceptable!"* a reality, there are three things we must do, and these three things are set forth in our text.

In our text the Psalmist says, *"Turn and depart from evil and do good; and then you will live securely, yes you will dwell in the land forever."* In this text there are three verbs that begin with the letter "**D**," and these three words provide the three steps we need to take. They are:

I.   **Depart**
II.   **Do**
III. **Dwell**

I.   **Depart**

Notice the word "**depart**" in our text. Professor Strong tells us it is the Hebrew word (*suwr*), and some other terms he provides in his Concordance that are suitable for translation are: "to decline; put away; remove; withdraw; and to be without."

So this word "depart" means to break away from, to block out, to concentrate, and to intensely focus.

During this past football season, Wes Byrum certainly employed this first principle when he kicked those last second field goals against Clemson, Kentucky and Oregon. He blocked out the crowd, he *departed* his mind from those distractions, and he kicked those field goals through the uprights.

Several years ago we had a young man who was also a kicker on the Auburn University football team, and he attended

91

our church. He became one of my good friends. His name is Jarret Holmes, and if I'm not mistaken, when he graduated from Auburn he kicked for the New York Giants in the NFL.

I remember I would go out and watch Jarret and the other players practice. I was especially intrigued by the kickers. If I ever played college football, I would want to be a kicker. They hardly ever get tackled. During practice, they just sort of get together as a group, gather under the goal post and talk to one another. Sometimes they will choose up and play a little touch football, and sometimes they will practice kicking the ball. It is interesting that, like the quarterbacks, they wear green jerseys. Those green jerseys mean that they are not to be tackled by anybody. I remember those kickers would look over at those big ole ugly defensive linemen as if to say, "Don't you get anywhere near me. I've got on this green jersey, and you can't mess with me. Ha! Ha!"

I remember it was the 1997 Iron Bowl when Auburn was playing the University of Alabama. I was serving as the chaplain with the football team, and I was on the sideline. It came down to the final seconds and a field goal attempt by Jarret. If he made the field goal, Auburn would win the West and would go to Atlanta and play the University of Tennessee in the SEC Championship Game.

Jarret lined up to kick the field goal, and Alabama called a time out. They lined up again, and Alabama called a second time out. They were trying to distract and get inside of Jarret's mind. But Jarret used those negatives as positives as he said a prayer each time, blocked out those 85,000 screaming fans, concentrated, and totally focused upon the ball. The snapper centered the ball and Jarret kicked it through the uprights, and Auburn won.

Now, just as Jarret blocked that crowd and those distracting thoughts from his mind, so we must *depart* from those negative thoughts and block them from our minds also. We must allow the Holy Spirit to stand as a Sentinel before our minds and let Him control and discipline any thoughts that seek to come into our minds.

And so the first step to make this statement a reality is to "**depart**" from the evil of those negative and destructive thoughts.

II.   Do

Notice our text goes on to say, *"...depart from evil and do good..."*

Again Dr. Strong reminds us that the Hebrew word we translate "do" is the word (*asah*), and other terms he lists in his Concordance that this word can mean are: "to be industrious; to labor; to perform."

John Wesley certainly understood the importance of this word as he said:

> *Do all the good you can;*
> *By all the means you can;*
> *In all the ways you can;*
> *In all the places you can;*
> *To all the people you can;*
> *At all the times you can;*
> *As long as ever you can.*

And I hope I got all of Brother Wesley's "cans" into that quotation. In other words, the way we defeat the evil of negativism in our life is to *do* good. It is to stay busy.

One of the fundamental laws of Psychology is that it is utterly impossible for any human mind to be positive and negative at the same time. No matter how brilliant you are, you can only think of one thing at a time.

You see, you cannot have negative thoughts in your mind when you are thinking positively and doing positive things, and any physician will tell you that one of the best antiseptics for sick nerves is to be positive and stay busy.

Alfred Lord Tennyson understood the value of this, for when he lost his most intimate friend Hallam, he cried, "I must lose myself in action, lest I wither in despair."

One of the fine young ladies in our church is Lauren Johnston. She went through our youth program, and she felt God's call upon her life to be a missionary to Ghana.

Lauren was home and she was visiting with Reverend Charles Cummings in his office. They walked out to her car, and Lauren noticed on the front seat that someone had placed some cheese sticks and chocolate chip cookies. Lauren got all excited and she started jumping up and down. Lauren had been a cheerleader, so she knew how to get excited and jump up and down.

Then she looked at Charles and with great wisdom she said, "If you are doing what God has called you to do, and you are where God has called you to be, then happiness and joy have a way of finding you."

And I might add, when that joy and happiness positively find you, then those negative evil enemies like worry and anxiety can find no place in your mind and life.

And so, after we **depart** from these evil thoughts, we then need to *do* good in a positive way.

III.   Dwell

Again, Dr. Strong tells us that the Hebrew word we translate "**dwell**" is (*shakan*), and he says that this word also means: "to rest; to remain; to reside, to permanently stay and to inhabit."

Do you remember under point one we said that the Holy Spirit should stand as a Sentinel before our minds and control and discipline the thoughts that seek to come into our minds. Well, not only should the Holy Spirit stand there, but we should bring Him into our lives and we should **dwell** within Him.

I remember as a little boy growing up in the First Methodist Church in Opelika, Alabama, in the Sunday night worship services, we would have hymn time where we would sing the old Gospel songs of the faith. I remember we would sing out of "The Spiritual Life" songbook and the "Cokesbury" song

94

book. How that singing ministered to me and helped me grow spiritually. It was very influential in shaping my theology. My dad would lead the singing.

I especially remember one hymn that we would sing quite often. It is entitled *Dwelling in Beulah Land*. I've thought a lot about that song, for you see, Beulah Land is representative of where God is, and we constantly need to **dwell** within Him.

I remember the chorus of that song goes:

> *I'm living on the mountain underneath a cloudless sky;*
> *I'm drinking from the fountain that never shall run dry;*
> *I'm feasting on the manna from a bountiful supply;*
> *For I am <u>dwelling</u> in Beulah Land.*

Notice the verb in the final line is **dwelling**, as we need to *dwell* in Beulah Land in the presence of our God.

I had a funeral in Tuskegee, Alabama, this past Friday. I got there early and drove out to Tuskegee University. You can see the influence of Dr. George Washington Carver all over that great school. Dr. George Washington Carver is one of my heroes.

It was 1921. Dr. Carver was summoned to Washington, D.C., to appear before the House Ways and Means Committee. They wanted him to explain his work on the commercial and medical value and potential of the peanut.

Now, keep in mind, this was in 1921. Dr. Carver arrived, and there were several speakers on the list. They placed his name last, and they made him wait all day.

He was the only African American in the room. All through the day he heard many bigoted and derisive comments. Some of them were meant to be funny, but they hurt and cut deeply for him. All through the day he felt uneasy and even terrified.

Finally his turn came, and he walked down the long aisle to the podium. As he walked, he felt the hate and hostility of many around him. As he approached the front, a committee member leaned back in his chair, and he put his feet up on the table and pulled his hat over his face indicating that he was going to sleep. When the chairman told the man to kindly take his feet from his desk and remove his hat, he responded with a racial slur.

Dr. Carver had a sick and sinking feeling in his stomach, and he was ready to turn around and go back home to Tuskegee, but instead he remembered two things. One, he remembered that he was a child of God. He said, "No matter what they say to me or how they treat me, I am a child of God." Two, he remembered that although there were anger and bitterness and hate and hostility all around him, he was **dwelling** in the presence of the Most High God. He was **dwelling** in Beulah Land, and there was a sweet peace on the inside.

With those two thoughts, he opened his briefcase, took out his materials, and he began his presentation. All who were present were impressed and inspired by what he had to say. They were impressed by his sincerity and kindness, but even more they were impressed by his competence and professionalism. He so captivated that committee, and after he had finished with his allotted 20 minutes, the chairman granted him 20 more minutes. The chairman asked for an extension of time, and there was no opposition to the request. Carver was given four additional extensions of time and spoke for several hours to an audience that hung on every word. At the conclusion of the presentation, every member of that committee stood and gave to Dr. George Washington Carver—a brilliant scientist and former slave—a long round of applause.

You see, earlier he could not keep the anger, bitterness and negativism from coming. I am reminded of these words by St. Francis of Assisi, "I can't stop the birds from flying over my head, but I can stop them from nesting in my hair." No, Dr. Carver could not keep that negativism from coming, but he **could** stop it from affecting him, and he did it by **dwelling** in the presence of the Most High.

And my friend, when angry, bitter, deadly, destructive, and negative thoughts come your way—notice I didn't say *"IF"* they come, but *"When"* they come—when they come your way and attack you, you say *"Not Acceptable"* and you defeat them with Psalm 37:27, as you *depart* from their evil, *do* good, and *dwell* in the land forevermore. Yes, you *dwell* in Beulah Land.

In closing, notice the theological and practical message in each of the verses in this hymn, and let's go out and live by them:

Far away the noise of strife upon my ear is falling,
Then I know the sins of earth beset on ev'ry hand;
Doubt and fear and things of earth in vain to me are calling,
None of these shall move me from Beulah Land.

Far below the storm of doubt upon the world is beating,
Sons of men in battle long the enemy withstand:
Safe am I within the castle of God's word retreating,
Nothing then can reach me— 'tis Beulah Land.

Let the stormy breezes blow, their cry cannot alarm me;
I am safely sheltered here, protected by God's hand:
Here the sun is always shining, here their's naught can
Harm me, I am safe forever in Beulah Land.

Viewing here the works of God, I sink in contemplation,
Hearing now His blessed voice, I see the way He planned:
Dwelling in the Spirit, here I learn of full salvation,
Gladly will I tarry in Beulah Land.

Chorus

I'm living on the mountain, underneath a cloudless sky,
I'm drinking at the fountain that never shall run dry;
O yes! I'm feasting on the manna from a bountiful supply,
For I am dwelling in Beulah Land.

Chapter 10

Love and Kindness Are the Most Important Things in the World
*"Mark (shamar) the perfect, the blameless (tam) man,
behold the upright; for the end of that man is peace."*
Psalm 37:37
Psalm 37:3-4; 27, 37
Fourth Sermon in Series: *Biblical Principles by Which I Daily Live*

I don't know when I've ever enjoyed preaching a series of sermons as much as this series on *Biblical Principles by Which I Daily Live*. It has challenged me to look deeply into my faith and mind and study the spiritual principles that are important to me—and how these principles govern my life and give theological purpose and practical direction each day.

I build my faith daily upon these four underpinning biblical principles, and they provide the foundation for my life. The first thing I do every morning is speak these principles aloud along with the biblical verses that give to them scriptural substance. All of the verses are taken from Psalm 37.

In these sermons, I want you to notice the congruous succession of these principles as they develop. The first principle is upward in its focus as we trust God. The second and third principles are inward in their direction as they help us choose to be happy within, and keep worry, stress and anxiety out of our lives. This fourth principle is outward in its application as it shows us how to relate to people in a loving and kind way.

You see, it's not enough to trust God and learn to live with ourselves. We must also learn to get along with people, for as we live life each day, we have to deal with people.

I have a friend who is a lawyer in Mobile, Alabama, and he told me one day, "George, I love being a lawyer. The only thing I don't like is having to work with people. They irritate me, and they annoy me. They don't do what I think they should do. People complicate life for me."

And that attorney is so correct. People can complicate life, and we do have to live with them. But as I live with them each day, I allow this fourth principle to come into effect, and the fourth principle is *Love and Kindness are the Most Important Things in the World.*

The text for this fourth sermon is Psalm 37:37. It is my conviction that this particular verse is a prophetic reference to Jesus Christ. It speaks of "the perfect man." There has been only one perfect man to have ever lived and that was Jesus, so I believe this is a reference to Him. This thought and interpretation first came to me during a colloquy session with other doctorial students at Vanderbilt Divinity School when a friend in the Disciples of Christ denomination shared a paper with our group he had written entitled *Pictures of the Christ in the Psalter.*

I want you to notice our text very carefully. The Psalmist says, **"Mark."** The Hebrew word we translate "mark" is the word *shamar.* Professor Strong in his Concordance tells us that this word means to "hedge about," it means "to watch and to observe." It means to "intently gaze upon."

And so the Psalmist tells us to "Mark the **perfect**...." Again I want you to notice the word that we translate as "blameless or perfect." Dr. Strong tells us it is the Hebrew word, *tam,* and he reminds us it is from the primitive Hebrew root, *tamâm.* He tells us that this word means "to accomplish and to consume." It means "to finish." And when I read it, I think of my Blessed Lord before He was crucified. He prayed to His Father in Heaven and said, "I have **accomplished** what You have given Me to do. I have **finished** My task."

I remember when I was at Yale, I was in a seminar and we were discussing the Christology of the Old Testament. I remember one of my colleagues referenced this particular verse as he said that this verse must be understood within the context of social justice. He postulated the view that inherent within Jesus is the ethic of love, and only this love can lead to peace. Now while I certainly agree with him, I also believe this verse has a deeper spiritual and practical application. The last word in the verse is "**peace**." The Hebrew word we translate peace is *shalom*, and in the Hebrew, the word *shalom* means more than the absence of war. It means the deep abiding presence of an inner serenity and tranquility.

And so, the Psalmist goes on to say, *"Mark the perfect man and behold the upright; for the end of that man is **peace**."*

Jesus was the very embodiment of peace and love, and out of that peace and love proceeded kindness for everybody. So thus, I contend that kindness out of a heart of love is the most important thing in the world, and this is a principle I seek to live by each day, and I seek to implement it in all of my relationships.

Against the background of this verse and this fourth principle, there are three ways I want us to consider kindness within the context of agape love. I want us to consider:

I.   **The Example for It**
II.   **The Expression of It**
III.   **The Expectation in It**

I.   **The Example for It**

Who is our example for kindness? There have been many kind people who are examples for me with their kindness.

I think of Kirk Wimberly, a classmate at Young Harris College. I remember Kirk made a big impression upon me. He was the President of the Student Body, and he was one of the kindest people I've ever met. I remember I was studying with Kirk one night and he said to me, "George, always have a big smile and a kind word for everybody—regardless of what they say to you or do to you." That arresting statement so ministered to me, and I wrote it in the front of my Bible, and I seek to live by it everyday.

I think of Cy Dawsey who was a retired Methodist

missionary from Brazil and such an important part of our church here in Auburn. Cy was one of the most Christlike people I've ever known, and his kindness warmed my heart.

I think of my own dad, Brother Si, and how he exuded kindness. Many times when I'm faced with a big decision I will ask myself, "How would my dad handle this?" Every time I think of him handling a situation, I always think of the kindness he would exhibit and how his ultimate decision would be made in a spirit of loving kindness.

Another example for kindness in my life is Dr. Roy Angell. Dr. Roy Angell was a Southern Baptist minister who many years ago was President of the Southern Baptist Convention. I never knew Dr. Angell, but I am so touched and moved by his example of kindness.

Leadership magazine told of when the Southern Baptist Convention many years ago held its annual meeting in Ft. Worth, Texas. Dr. Angell flew to Ft. Worth, and he checked into his hotel. It was a stormy night, and it was pouring down rain. The Convention was to convene the next morning. The Convention Center was not far from the hotel where Dr. Angell was staying, so he decided to walk down to the Convention Hall and look around. (I remember in 2008 when I attended the General Conference of The United Methodist Church. It was held at the very same Convention Center in Ft. Worth.) That evening there was, as *Leadership* magazine described him, an ardent Texas fundamentalist by the name of J. Frank Norris.

He thought the Southern Baptist Church was a liberal tool of the Devil. He had set up a small speaking platform by the Convention Center, and he was espousing the evils of the Southern Baptist Church. As he spoke, he was getting wet by the pouring rain.

Rev. Norris and Dr. Angell had never met each other. As Norris spoke, Dr. Roy Angell stepped up to the small platform and stood behind him. He placed his umbrella over Norris, and he gently placed his hand upon the shoulder of Norris. As he did, Norris spoke even more heatedly of the evils of the Southern

Baptist Convention and especially its diabolical leader, Dr. C. Roy Angell. Finally, when Norris was finished, he turned and thanked his generous benefactor for his kindness, never knowing that the person holding the umbrella was Dr. Roy Angell. Yes, what an example for me is Dr. Roy Angell!

But as much as I appreciate Kirk Wimberly and Cy Dawsey and Si Mathison, and Roy Angell, they are not my ultimate example. The one upon whom I look for my example is Jesus Christ.

It is interesting that the Greek word for "Christ" is the word χριστος. The Greek word for "kind" is χρεστος. Notice that only one letter separates Christ from kindness, and I've found that the closer I am to my Christ, the kinder I am to His children.

Yes, Christ is our example for kindness.

II.   The Expression of It

Now to whom are we to express this kindness? We are to express it to everybody. Ephesians 4:32 begins by saying, *"Be kind to one another."* The Greek word we translate as "to one another" is ἀλλήλους, and it is a term that is inclusive of everybody, and I might point out that all around us are people who are yearning and longing for the kindness we have to express.

Dr. Ellsworth Kalas served as the President of Asbury Theological Seminary. Dr. Kalas said this about kindness:

> *A psychiatrist pondered the state of the world as he came to the end of a long, difficult day. He had dealt with both violence and apathy, with a young woman who saw no reason to go on living, and with a man who was sure he could never put his life together. Some of the problems were the result, he reasoned, of chemical imbalance or of physical ailments; but as he reviewed his day, and compared it with most*

other days and with the experience of his colleagues in psychiatry, he offered an estimate: at least half of those who are mentally ill could have been spared their illness by simple human kindness.

This challenges us to understand that the time to do kindness, to think it, to speak it, is now. If it is true, that more than half of the mentally ill could have been spared their illness by "simple human kindness," then how many other lesser pains could be avoided—and how much more happiness could be wrought—if only each of us could share a bit more kindness? The demand is still far greater than the supply.

This is the day to be kind. Tomorrow will be too, and so will the next day. But today is the day to be born again in kindness; for you and I won't pass this way again.

Henry James, an American author who lived in the last century, said, "Three things in human life are important. The first is to be kind. The second is to be kind. The third is to be kind."

And so, our challenge is to express this kindness.

III.   The Expectation in It

If out of a heart of love you are kind to people, then you can expect certain benefits and blessings. When you are kind, you in return will be blessed.

You will be blessed socially. When you are kind you will have more friends. You will truly know the joy of winning friends and influencing people. You will be popular in your fraternity and in your sorority. You will be popular in your social circles. People gravitate towards kindness, but on the other hand, nothing will alienate you from people any more than to be unkind. Folks do not enjoy being around unkind people, but when you are kind you will, as Dale Carnegie says, "Win friends and influence people."

Yes, it will bless you socially.

Also, it will bless you professionally. It will benefit you with your job and with your vocation. If you want to be successful in your chosen profession, then there are several things you need.

First, you need a good **education**. You need to be well prepared.

Secondly, you need **experience**. Experience is a valuable commodity in the work place.

Thirdly, you need **expertise**. When you are knowledgeable in your field, it will pay great dividends.

But I dare say that as important as these three factors are, a fourth factor that is just as important is kindness. Kindness will help you with your job as nothing else. It will help you progress, and it will help you gain the confidence of those who work over you and under you. Yes, kindness will bring results in a way that nothing else can.

It was a cold winter night in Philadelphia. A dear elderly man and woman made their way into a small hotel seeking lodging for the night. The clerk at the hotel was a young man named George Boldt.

The elderly man approached him and asked if he had a vacant room. Mr. Boldt responded by saying, "I'm so sorry, but because of the many conventions in town we are full."

The elderly man and his wife very dejectedly turned and started to walk into the freezing night of snow and sleet. As they turned to leave, Mr. Boldt walked up and put his arms on both of their shoulders and said, "I cannot send a nice couple like you into the rain at one o'clock in the morning. Would you be willing to sleep in my room?"

They took the young man's room and they lodged there for the night.

The next morning when the elderly man paid his bill, he said to young Boldt, "You are the type of young man who needs to manage a large hotel. My wife and I have been so inspired and impressed by your kindness. Maybe someday I will build that hotel for you!" As he said that, his wife with a gleam in her eye looked at Mr. Boldt and smiled knowingly. They had a good laugh over the elderly man's extravagant remark. Mr. Boldt helped them as they made their way to a cab outside the hotel.

Two years later, Mr. Boldt received a letter with a round trip train ticket instructing him to come to New York right away. The note told George Boldt where to meet this elderly man. They met in New York City at the appointed place, and then the elderly man took Mr. Boldt to the corner of 34th Street and 5th Avenue. There they stood, and the elderly man pointed to what seemed like the grandest hotel in New York City. It was a palace of reddish stone with turrets and watch towers. It was like a castle from a medieval fairyland reaching into the sky.

The elderly man of distinction looked at the young man and said, "That is the hotel I have just built for you to manage." And then tears came to his eyes and a big lump to his throat as he said, "I have never forgotten your kindness to my wife and me that cold night in Philadelphia. That meant more to me than anything in the world. Not a day has gone by that I have not thought about that. I want you to manage this hotel. We are calling it the Waldorf Astoria Hotel. By the way, my name is William Waldorf Astoria."

No, you never know the benefits and blessings your kindness will render in the work place.

And kindness will bless your family. I believe one of the greatest needs within the home today is kindness. It is simply for husbands and wives to learn to be kind to each other. It is for children and parents to learn to be kind to one another. Kindness can heal a multitude of hurts.

Finally, it will bless you personally. It is my belief that the greatest benefit and blessing of kindness will be personal for you. You see, kindness is very therapeutic. When you are kind, not only do you bless others, but that blessing comes back to you several fold, and it brings an inner peace. The one thing so many of us are looking for in life is peace. Notice again our text, and especially the last word as it says, *"Mark the perfect man, behold the upright; for the end of that man is **peace.**"*

I'll challenge you to treat everybody you meet with love and kindness—and in so doing you will experience this blessed **peace** within your life.

Biblical Principles by Which I Daily Live! Every day that I live, I trust God; I choose to be happy; I do not allow negativism into my life; and I seek to be kind to everybody I meet. What a way to live! I'll challenge you to join me as we live this exciting and wonderful and fulfilled life together!

Section III

Comforting Thoughts

Chapter 11

"The Fixer"

"The Spirit of the Lord is upon Me because He has...sent Me to proclaim freedom to the prisoners, to heal, to fix, the brokenhearted..."
Luke 4:18a
Luke 4:16-19

One of my best pals in our church is Linda Tigney. I love and appreciate her so much. I am especially blessed by the deep faith she reflects from her rich and beautiful African American tradition. It does me good just to be around her. Her big smile, her sweet spirit, her bright enthusiasm and her genuine love for her Lord and people are an inspiration to my life and ministry. One of the real joys of my ministry was when she was appointed to serve her first church in this Annual Conference. Brother Charles and I both preached for her and she is greatly loved by her congregation.

One day she and I were talking about Jesus and the many names ascribed to Him. We spoke of the names that are especially meaningful during this Advent season as we recalled how Isaiah prophesied that His Name would be called "Wonderful, Counselor, the Mighty God, the Everlasting Father and the Prince of Peace." We also spoke of how Luke records in chapter 1:78 that Jesus is referred to as the "Dayspring from on High."

And then we reflected upon the names that Jesus gave Himself in the Book of John. He said, "I am the Bread of Life; I am the Light of the World; I am the Door; I am the Good Shepherd; I am the Resurrection and the Life; I am the Way, the Truth and the Life; I am the True Vine." Jesus is called the "Rose of Sharon" and the "Lily of the Valley." He is also called the "Fairest of Ten Thousand" and the "Bright and Morning Star." Jesus is our Savior, our Redeemer, our Sanctifier and our Coming King, and He is called The Great Physician.

And then Linda looked at me, and I remember there was such a glow about her countenance, such a sweetness in her spirit, such a twinkle in her eyes and such a deep spiritual conviction in her voice as she said, "Brother George, first and foremost, my Jesus is 'The Fixer.' He can *fix* anything."

In all of my theological readings in the areas of Christology and Soteriology; in all of my theological studies from Emory, Vanderbilt, Sewanee and Yale, I don't believe I had ever heard a description that so beautifully and powerfully encapsulates why Jesus came into this world and what He came to do. That statement so eloquently describes His being, His nature and His purpose.

Yes, "My Jesus is **The Fixer**, and He can **fix** anything that is broken." And that is exactly how our Lord described His purpose for coming into the world. In Luke 4:18 we observe Jesus as He was standing in the synagogue in Nazareth reading from the Book of Isaiah. He spoke the words of our text when He said in verse 18, "The Spirit of the Lord is upon Me because He has sent Me to preach deliverance to the captives and prisoners, and **to heal the brokenhearted**."

We are living in a world of brokenness. Henri Nouwen in his book, *Bread for the Journey* writes *"Our life is full of brokenness—broken relationships, broken promises, broken expectations. How can we live with that brokenness without becoming bitter and resentful, except by returning again and again to God's faithful presence in our lives."*

We have been doing a series of sermons on *Good People in Bad Places*. At one of our recent staff meetings our minister of congregational care, Julie Hare, shared with us that during this holiday season we need to realize that so many people in our congregation are hurting and they are daily dealing with grief. It was this statement by Julie that gave to me the inspiration to preach this sermon that I feel is so needed in our congregation during this holiday season. In this sermon I want to lift up *three areas* of brokenness where our Lord can bring wholeness. I want to mention *three areas* of hurt where Jesus can bring healing. Yes, I want to mention *three areas* of brokenness that our Savior can "*fix*."

This morning, He wants to bring healing and wholeness and *fix* our:

I. Broken Relationships
II. Broken Minds
III. Broken Hearts

I. Broken Relationships

One of the sad things about life is that relationships that are so seemingly very strong can so easily be broken—relationships among colleagues, compatriots, teammates, friends and family members—and yes even husbands and wives.

When I counsel with couples who are preparing for marriage, in my premarital counseling I always share with them that the two most important parts of a marriage are:

Secondly, communication. Communication is so very important. Most problems in your marriage will arise because of a lack of communication. That is why it is so important that you learn to communicate with each other.

In my premarital counseling I always give couples a little workbook that is entitled *Getting Ready for Marriage Workbook: How to Really Get to Know the Person You're Going to Marry*. It takes the entire marriage experience and breaks it down into ten areas. There is a little test for each of them to take at the end of each chapter. Without consulting each other, they take the test and then they compare notes. It asks questions that quite often they don't how to ask each other or do not feel comfortable asking each other, but in knowing the answers, it will help them communicate more effectively, and it will help them truly get to know each other better. In every instance couples have told me how much fun it was doing that workbook because it dealt only with the two of them and their lives. Every time, they always tell me that it helped them learn to communicate better.

But *first*, and by far, the most important part of a marriage is trust. It is so important that a couple trusts each other. I always tell couples that the trust factor is the most important part of their marriage, and I implore them to guard that sacred bond of trust. If it is ever broken, with God's grace it can be restored—but it is hard. That is why they need to guard it with their lives. But it can be broken.

It happened to Gordon MacDonald.

Gordon was the pastor of Grace Chapel in Lexington, Massachusetts, which is the largest Protestant church in New England. He then became President of InterVarsity Christian Fellowship. Gordon had written a best selling book entitled *Ordering Your Private World*. It is a wonderful theological study of how we can conform our wills with the will and way of Christ.

But then Gordon's private world fell apart and broke into pieces. He had an affair with another woman. He resigned from his church and from InterVarsity, and he withdrew from public ministry.

His wife Gail and he went to their summer home, a little cottage, in New Hampshire. There they spent a year as they prayed together and studied the Bible together. They invited some dear and trusted friends into their home to counsel with them and share spiritual direction.

Over that year, the forgiveness and healing power of Christ brought them back together, and he was given a second chance. Ministers don't always get a second chance.

He was called to serve a small congregation in New York City, and then he was called to return to Grace Chapel in Massachusetts. He and his wife Gail were welcomed with open hearts and open arms. Gordon then wrote another book, and he entitled this book *Rebuilding Your Broken World*. In the introduction, he shares these moving words:

...I am a broken—world person...for the rest of my life, I will have to live with the knowledge that I brought deep sorrow to my wife, to my children, and to my friends and others who have trusted me for many years...As Gail and I rebuilt our broken worlds...the process...centered on the acts of repentance, forgiveness, grace and a new chosen direction of performance. And it has provided us a costly love that has bonds of steel.

It is interesting to note that this book was written in 1988, and some ten years later somebody gave a copy of it to Bill Clinton, the President of the United States. It was Gordon MacDonald and two other pastors who visited and counseled with Bill Clinton at the White House and helped him and Hillary Clinton rebuild their own broken world.

Yes, my Savior can heal and *fix* broken relationships.

II.   Broken Minds

James 1:8, says "A double minded man is unstable in all his ways." That is an interesting phrase in the Greek. The verse begins with the two Greek words ***anar dipsukos*** (ἀνὴρ δίψυχος), and it is a reference to a person's mind that is broken.

You see, when God made our minds He made them to be unified entities, and when our minds are divided, we cannot control them.

That is what Horace meant when he said, "Rule your mind or your mind will rule you."

And the reason so many people are not happy during this holiday season is because their minds are scattered and broken by worry and anxiety and stress, and their minds are torn in many different directions.

I think the perfect biblical illustration of this second point is Mark 5.

Jesus and the disciples had been in the midst of the Sea of Galilee, and they encountered a terrible storm. They came to the other side of the sea to a place called the "Land of the Gadarenes." As soon as the ship landed, a man ran out of a cemetery who must have frightened the disciples. He was a pitiful looking creature. He was naked. He was bound with chains, physical chains that bound his body, but even worse, mental chains that bound his mind. He was crying and bleeding as he had been cutting himself. And then Jesus, *The Fixer*, changed his life. He extracted from him all of that evil. He put the evil into some

112

swine, and the swine ran into the sea.

In verse 15, we have a beautiful picture as it says "And he was clothed and in his right mind," and that is what our Savior does when our minds are broken and shattered. He touches them with His healing grace, and He brings wholeness and peace.

III.   Broken Hearts

I love to study the Psalms. There are 150 Psalms, and I prayerfully read a Psalm early each morning. Dietrich Bonhoeffer said, "The Psalter (The Book of Psalms) is my prayer book." And like Bonhoeffer, the Psalter is my prayer book also.

I love to take a Psalm each day, pray over that Psalm, study it and exegete the words from the Hebrew. With each Psalm, I will give a title, find a key verse and then outline it.

This past week I was studying Psalm 147, and I personally entitled that Psalm, *God's Cure for a Broken Heart*. As I carefully studied that Psalm, I found and outlined six beautiful and practical ways that God can heal our broken hearts.

The key verse to that Psalm is verse 3 as it says, "He heals the brokenhearted, and He binds up their wounds."

I wonder how many broken hearts are in this service today. I wonder how many broken hearts are in our community during this holiday season?

Oh, the Good News of the Gospel is that we worship a Savior who longs to bring wholeness and to heal and to **fix** our broken hearts. All we have to do is bring to Him that brokenness and strife, and He will indeed bring healing to our lives.

Bill Gaither reminds us of this truth in his beautiful song. As we listen to it, lets allow God's healing grace to work within our hearts.

If there ever were dreams
That were lofty and noble,
They were my dreams at the start;
And hope for life's best were the hopes
That I harbor down deep in my heart;
But my dreams turned to ashes,
And my castles all crumbled,
My fortune turned to loss,
So I wrapped it all in the rags of life,
And laid it at the cross.

Something beautiful, something good;
All my confusion He understood.
All I had to offer Him was brokenness and strife;
But he made something beautiful of my life.

Chapter 12

The Thirteenth Commandment
"Do not worry (μεριμνᾶτε) about anything..."
Philippians 4:6a
Philippians 4:6-8

John Wesley said, "Before I can preach grace, I must first preach the law," for we do not realize our need for grace until we see our inability to keep the law.

Of course, the ultimate law is the Decalogue or what we know as The Ten Commandments.

God thundered down to Moses on Mount Sinai in Exodus 20, and gave to him these Ten Commandments.

You may remember, back about eleven years ago we did a series of sermons on The Ten Commandments as we devoted a sermon to each one of them and studied each individual commandment in-depth.

You are familiar with The Ten Commandments:
You shall have no other gods before Me; You shall not make before me any graven image; You shall not take the name of the Lord your God in vain; Remember the Sabbath day to keep it holy.—Now it is interesting to note as you study The Ten Commandments, these first four have to do with our relationship to God while the final six have to do with our relationship with other people—*Honor your father and your mother; You shall not steal; You shall not kill; You shall not commit adultery; You shall not bear false witness;* and *You shall not covet.*

When I finished doing those ten sermons I realized that in Matthew 22 there are two other commandments, for in that chapter a lawyer approached Jesus and said to Him, "What is the greatest commandment?" Jesus responded by saying, "The greatest commandment is for you to love the Lord your God with all your heart, soul and mind." Now, that first commandment in the New

Testament is in actuality the 11th Commandment.

Then Jesus continued by saying, "And the second commandment is like it—you are to love your neighbor as yourself." And so, this second commandment would be the 12th Commandment, and so up to this point we actually have Twelve Commandments.

And then I was studying Philippians 4:6, which is our text, and I realized there is a 13th Commandment as Paul says, "Do not worry..."

Now, I want you to note that this is not a recommendation, and it is not a suggestion. It is a commandment as Paul says, "Do not worry....," and here Paul is simply echoing the words of Jesus in the Sermon on the Mount when our Lord said, "Do not worry or be anxious about tomorrow."

As I reflect upon these thirteen commandments I realize that we all do a pretty good job of keeping the first ten commandments. I don't know of many people who steal, or kill, or break those other commandments.

We do a pretty good job of keeping the 11th Commandment as we do love God with all of our heart, soul and mind, but we do not do quite as good a job with the 12th Commandment when Jesus tells us to love our neighbor as ourselves. You see, sometimes it can be hard to love our neighbors, especially if our neighbors are obnoxious, and obstreperous, and ornery—but we still do a pretty fair job of keeping this 12th Commandment.

But, for most of us, we do a lousy job of keeping the 13th Commandment. The Bible plainly tells us not to worry, but yet many of us do worry.

One of the most tender of stories in all of Holy Scripture is found in Luke 10. Jesus entered the home in Bethany of Mary, Martha and Lazarus. He observed Martha and He said in verse 41, "Martha, you are worried and you are anxious about many things." And so, when we worry, we are in pretty good company because Martha, who was so close to Jesus, worried also.

The questions which I want to pose in this sermon are: "How can we defeat the enemy of worry in our lives? How can we overcome and solve the problem of anxiety?"

I want to suggest to you three simple steps, and if you will take these steps, they will put your feet on the roadway to living a worry-free life.

The three steps are:

I. Forget the Past
II. Live in the Present
III. Place the Future

I. Forget the Past

In the Book of Philippians Paul says, "This one thing I do forgetting...." And like Paul, we need to forget.

I enjoy that great theologian, Lou Holtz. You are familiar with Lou as he is a commentator on ESPN. He has a segment called "Dr. Lou." It begins with the repetitive statements, "Dr. Lou, Dr. Lou, Dr. Lou..." and then someone will say, "The Doctor is in." And then Dr. Lou will pontificate with some athletic axiom of motivation, intermingling a little bit of philosophy and theology with the thought. When he finishes, the person will say, "The Doctor is Out." I'm not sure where he is out to, but he is out.

I've heard him many times, and half the time I have difficulty understanding him, but I appreciate his "down-home" philosophy. In one of the presentations he said, "Happiness is no more than a poor memory. Happiness is forgetting."

Now I partially agree with Lou. While I don't think happiness is a poor memory, I do believe happiness is a selective memory. We need to be selective about the things we remember, and we need to be selective about the things we forget.

Some people have selective hearing. They hear what they want to hear. You know folks like that. You may be married to somebody like that.

I read about a wealthy old man who was hard of hearing. He lived with his family. One day he decided to get a hearing aid, and the ear doctor told him about a hearing aid that was so small that it would be completely concealed and no one would ever know he was wearing it. The man bought the hearing aid.

Two weeks later he saw the doctor, and the doctor asked how he was enjoying his hearing aid. The man replied, "It is great and it is wonderful. I love it."

The doctor then said, "How do your family members like it?" The man looked at the doctor and said, "Oh, they don't even know I have it, and I am having the time of my life. I've already changed my will three times in the last two days."

Yes, like selective hearing, we need to have a selective memory, and we need to be selective about what we forget.

You see, you don't need to forget everything. You remember those thoughts that are dear and precious to your heart. We sing that old Gospel song,

> **Precious memories how they linger,**
> **How they ever flood my soul,**
> **In the stillness of the midnight,**
> **Precious, sacred scenes unfold.**

Those precious memories that are so dear, you fold them up and you file them away in your memory, and you constantly refer to them for moments of happiness and joy.

But there are some things in the past that you need to forget.

One, we need to forget our mistakes. We all make mistakes. I make mistakes, and you make mistakes. We are imperfect people in an imperfect world, and we are going to make mistakes. Sometimes I wake up in the morning and I wonder, "What mistakes will I make today?" We try so hard, but yet we fail so miserably, and we make mistakes and we do foolish things.

In this message we are talking about worry, and the best book I've ever read on worry is a book by Dale Carnegie entitled *How to Stop Worrying and Start Living*. In this book, Mr. Carnegie tell us that we are going to make mistakes and do foolish things. Carnegie says that he has a file and written across the file are three letters: **F. T. D.** which stand for "Foolish Things I have

Done." And all of us have done foolish things, but the problem is that we are letting those foolish things we did in the past rob us of our happiness in the present. You just put those mistakes behind you and forget them. Yes, learn from them, but then forget them.

Two, we need to forget our sins.

There is a difference between a mistake and sin. A mistake is something we do accidentally, but a sin is a conscious act we commit that hurts God and other people. And like mistakes, we all commit sin. The Apostle Paul said, "Christ came into the world to save sinners of whom I am chief." And I know Brother Paul has a lot of co-chiefs who are standing right along beside him, and I am one of them.

But, we do sin. We all feel that downward pull. We understand well the words of that hymn,

Prone to wonder,
Lord I feel it.
Prone to leave,
The God I love.

Yes, we commit sin, but when we do, we need to ask God to forgive us, and when God forgives us He not only forgives, but He forgets. He remembers that sin no more.

Is there some sin you've committed in the past, and like a ball and chain you've carried that sin through life with you? Friend, just forget it; if God doesn't remember it anymore, why are you hanging onto it? You commit it to God and forget it and put it behind you.

We need to forget our sins.

Three, we need to forget our regrets.

We all have regrets, and I do not know of anything that can rob us of our happiness any more than our regrets.

Now, with your regrets, there are two things you need to do: **First**, if you can do something about that regret, do it. A man said to his minister, "The great regret of my life is that I never got a college degree. I wish so much I had. I regret it more than anything in the world." His minister said to him, "Well, why don't you go back and get your college degree."

The man said, "Reverend, I am thirty-five years of age, and going to school at night, it would take me ten years to get that degree."

The minister then asked the man this question, "How old will you be when you go back to school and get that degree?" The man replied, "Why, I will be forty-five years of age."

And then the minister asked the question, "How old will be you be if you don't go back and get it?" The man with a quizzical expression upon his face said, "I'll be forty-five. Why the same?"

Friend, if you can do something about that regret, you do it.

Secondly, if you can't do anything about that regret, then you block it out of your mind, forget it, and focus upon all the many positives in your life and all you do have going for you. But the important thing is to forget it.

And so the first step to eliminating the worry in your life is to learn to forget the past.

II.   Live in the Present

Learn to live today.

I am told that the song, *One Day At A Time, Sweet Jesus*, is the theme song for Alcoholics Anonymous. They know they can't live in the past, and they can't live in the future. They must take life **one day** at a time.

A few years ago I preached a sermon on the first Sunday of the year on the subject, "How to Live this New Year One Day at a Time." I remember after that message a dear friend came up, took me aside and spoke to me. This dear friend is battling the demon of addiction. I never will forget how he said with tears in his eyes, "Dr. Mathison, the only way I can be cured of this terrible disease is to take life one day at a time. And you know, I find that quite often I have to take it just one minute at the time, and I've found that living in the present is the only thing I can do to solve this problem."

I read about a caring physician who was visiting an elderly woman who was his patient. She was preparing for hip surgery. The doctor was very kind and compassionate, (and I just want to say how much I appreciate all the fine physicians in our church...not only are they the very best with their medical expertise, but I appreciate so much the kindness and compassion they have for their patients).

This dear elderly lady was anticipating the surgery, and she was very anxious and nervous. She said to the doctor, "Doctor, how long will I have to be here?"

The physician with a warm smile on his face tenderly put his arm around the dear lady and said, "Just one day at a time, my dear. One day at a time."

She responded, "Thank you, Doctor. I don't believe I could handle a month. I don't even think I could handle a week. But I know I can handle a day."

We prayed the Lord's Prayer a few moments ago, and did you notice the phrase, "Give us this day our daily bread." Notice that Jesus doesn't tell us to worry about the stale bread left over from yesterday. He doesn't tell us to fret about the wheat in the field and worry if there will be enough wheat to make bread tomorrow, but He simply focuses upon the bread today—"Give us this day, our daily bread."

And so, to eliminate the worry in your life, live in the present. Live right now. You see, this present moment is all you *have*. Today is all you have. Yesterday is gone, and tomorrow is not here. You throw this day away, and you throw away everything you have. You live just today, and you use everything you've got. Today is all you have.

Today is all you can **handle.** I was watching a fellow on television, and he was a juggler. He had several balls going at one time. Now that fellow can keep several balls going at one time, but you can't keep several days going at one time, but you can wreck your health trying. Don't try to juggle all the mistakes, and sins, and regrets of yesterday along with the uncertainties and fears of tomorrow. You just live this day. You just live this very moment. Today is all you have.

And today is all you **need**. Right now in this worship service, it is all you need to nurture the deep spiritual recesses of your soul. This day is all you need to mend a quarrel, to make a friend, to walk more closely with your Lord.

So, to defeat the enemy of worry, you live in the present.

III.   Place the Future

Now where do you need to **place** the future? You need to place it in God's hands, and you need to do it for two reasons. One, His hands are bigger than your hands, and they can handle anything you put in them. Two, those hands can sustain any burden that you give to Him.

The Psalmist says in Psalm 55:22, *"Cast your burden upon the Lord, and He will sustain you."*

One of my closest friends in the ministry was Bill Hinson. Bill followed Dr. Charles Allen as the pastor of the First United Methodist Church in Houston, Texas, which at that time was the largest church in our denomination.

Bill retired from that church and moved to Huntsville, Alabama, to be near his son and his grandchildren whom he dearly adored.

Bill and I were in seminary together, and we developed a very close relationship. We ate dinner together most every evening, and we studied together. I learned to love him like a brother. I preached for him in his churches, and enjoyed so much being with him and his wife, Jean.

The last time I was with Bill was at the General Conference at Pittsburgh. He died shortly after that Conference.

I had a very interesting thing happen in our church about a month ago. I mentioned Bill's name, and in an illustration I referenced one of his books. After the service a beautiful young girl came up to me, took me by the hand, and with a full throat said, "I am Bill Hinson's granddaughter. I am a freshman here at

Auburn, and I am from Huntsville."

I remember going to hear Bill preach at the Vinings United Methodist Church in Atlanta, Georgia, when we were in seminary at Emory. I remember how his message meant so much to me. I took notes, and I wrote down an illustration he shared. I found it in some old files that I was going through, and I was touched again by this illustration.

Bill told of a geography professor who went into a bookstore to purchase a globe to help him in the teaching task. He bought a globe about four feet tall. The professor had parked his pickup truck about two blocks from the bookstore. After purchasing the globe, he balanced it upon his shoulders, and he walked out of the store onto the busy street, making his way to his truck. He was struggling beneath the load of that globe.

He passed two elderly ladies who were staring at him. One lady said to the other one, "Look at that poor man. Trying to carry the weight of the world on his shoulders."

And I wonder if perhaps the good Lord is not looking into this sanctuary today at those of us here, and I wonder if He's not saying, "Look at that poor man, trying to carry the load of the world upon his shoulders. Look at that poor woman, trying to carry the load of the world upon her shoulders. Look at that college student, trying to carry the load of the world upon his shoulders."

Dear friend, whatever that load might be, you take it and you put it in the strong Hands of God.

In closing, may I ask you some questions, "When you came into this sanctuary today, were you worrying about some sin or mistake of the past? Were you bearing some heavy burden? Were you dealing with some terrible stress? Were you harboring some fear of the future? Were you coping with some anxiety? Were you carrying some worry?"

If so, I'll challenge you right now to take that burden, that stress, that fear, that anxiety, and that worry—and you place them in the Hands of God.

And if you do, I promise you that He will take care of you and be with you. Better yet, He promises.